"I wish to recommned *Spirituality and Science: Greek, Judeo-Christian and Islamic Perspectives* as a helpful text explaining the contributions of representatives from the monotheistic faith traditions to the evolution of Greek and Arabic science during its formative period in the medieval world. Beginning students and scholars will benefit greatly from reading this excellent book. The material includes informative discussions of Qur'anic verses as they related to the physical sciences. Arab/Muslim contributions in the fields of astronomy, chemistry and medicine were well described in this book. This book will expand understanding of the Arab/Muslim contributions to the global scientific enterprises of this era in conjunction with those of Jewish and Christian scholars as well."

Sami Ibrahim
Science Faculty
San Jose City College

Spirituality and Science: Greek, Judeo-Christian and Islamic Perspectives

---

Authors

Gerald Grudzen, M.Th., Ph.D.

Department of Philosophy

San Jose City College, San Jose, CA

In collaboration with Shamsur Rahman, Ph.D.

Commonwealth Visiting Fellow

Harris Manchester College, University of Oxford, UK

authorHOUSE®

AuthorHouse™ LLC
1663 Liberty Drive
Bloomington, IN 47403
www.authorhouse.com
Phone: 1-800-839-8640

Published by AuthorHouse   09/26/2014

ISBN: 978-1-4343-4236-2 (sc)

This book is printed on acid-free paper.

Table of Contents

Preface

Cosmic Spirituality

The environmental movement has brought about a renewed appreciation for the interdependency of all forms of life on the planet and taught us that the atomistic and mechanistic theories of the Cartesian and Newtonian eras were inadequate and incomplete explanations of the cosmos.

Our study, *Spirituality and Science: Greek, Judeo-Christian and Islamic Perspectives*, is an analysis of these three intellectual traditions as they influenced and impacted the Scientific Revolution of the sixteenth and seventeenth centuries. In our introduction, we discuss the need for a more holistic understanding of the relationship between spirituality and science, particularly in our understanding of man's relationship with nature. The environmental movement has brought about a renewed appreciation for the interdependency of all forms of life on the planet and taught us that the atomistic and mechanistic theories of the Cartesian and Newtonian eras were inadequate and incomplete explanations of the cosmos. A new relationship between spirituality and science is slowly emerging that unites rather than divides human life from other living beings (animal and plant life), man and the physical universe (the evolving cosmos), and the world of facts (science) and the world of meaning (religion and mythology). In Chapter One, we investigate the meaning of "experimental science" from an Islamic perspective, followed by an analysis of the Christian absorption and interpretation of Arabic philosophy and science in the thirteenth and fourteenth centuries. In the second chapter, we show the Greek roots of many of the philosophical and scientific concepts that engaged both Christian and Islamic scholars in the Middle Ages. Chapter Three discusses the Christian understanding of faith and healing during the New Testament era with special focus on the miracles of Jesus. Chapter Four discusses the Greco-Roman medical tradition inspired by the Hippocratic Corpus and the central contribution to medical thought found in the writings of Galen. As part of this analysis, we will show how, in the eleventh and twelfth centuries, monastic medicine played a central role in the reintroduction of Greco-Roman and Arabic medical texts into the West.

In the fifth chapter, we discuss the Greek philosophical tradition and its impact on the evolution of the Christian faith. In Chapter Six, we examine Islam and experimental science, along with the key philosophical and scientific contributions of Islamic scholars to astronomy, chemistry, medicine and optics. All of these philosophical and scientific developments were critical for the formation of a scientific culture that led to the Scientific Revolution, which inspired the discoveries of Copernicus, Galileo, Kepler and Descartes during the sixteenth and seventeenth centuries.

On the basis of this study, we show how Jewish, Muslim and Christian scholars contributed to the growth of a critical philosophy and scientific method during the Middle Ages. We wish to highlight the influence of Islamic scholars upon Christian philosophers and theologians of the Middle Ages and show that it was clearly substantial and integral to the evolution of scientific methods and logic. In the chapters that follow, we will highlight various and specific aspects of Muslim contributions to the rise of medical science in the West.

Although the Qu'ran[1] is not a book of science, it has its own style of dealing with the facts and principles of science. It deals with many presuppositions about scientific thinking and makes a number of suggestive statements regarding many phenomena, hinting at certain important organizing principles. For this reason, we will look at the holy Qu'ran to see whether its teachings are compatible with the concepts of modern science.

In the chapter on early Christianity, we also show the compatibility of Christian theology with Greek philosophy around the concepts of Faith and Reason. Some scholars claim that there is an irreconcilable conflict between knowledge and belief. They claim that belief should be replaced by knowledge; otherwise, it is mere superstition. Einstein tried to reconcile this conflict between belief and knowledge (religion and science). He thought that this conflict was unnecessary. He suggested that science can only ascertain what "is," not what "should be," and outside of its domain, value judgments of all kinds remain necessary. Religion, on the other hand, deals primarily with the evaluation and meaning of human thought and action. Science cannot adequately speak of facts and of relationships between facts without including the meanings associated with them. According to this interpretation, the well-known conflicts between religion and science in the past may be ascribed to a misapprehension of the respective domains of religion and science.[2]

Ascribing the conflict between science and religion as being due to misapprehension, Einstein brings out a possible conciliatory position existing between the two domains. He maintains that the realms of religion and science are clearly marked off from one another; nevertheless, there exist between the two strong reciprocal relationships and dependencies. Though religion may be that which determines the goal, it has, nevertheless, been informed by science. In the broadest sense, some of the means by which the attainment of the goals religion has established for itself, for example, in the moral sphere, have been through scientific developments. But those who seek the truth through science are often thoroughly imbued with the aspiration towards wisdom and understanding. This source of feeling and search for truth, however, springs from the sphere of religion. To this end, there also belongs the "faith" that science is likely to reveal valid truths for the world of existence and that these rules are rational, that is, comprehensible by reason. As Einstein once said, "I cannot conceive of a genuine scientist without that profound faith. The situation may be expressed by an image: science without religion is lame; religion without science is blind."[3] Throughout this text we will attempt to show that a conciliatory position has predominated in the history of religion and science from the time of the classical Greek philosophers through the absorption of this philosophical and scientific tradition within Christianity, followed by the translation of Greek texts and interpretation of them by Islamic, Jewish and Christian scholars in the Middle Ages. It should be noted that an educated elite of Jewish, Christian and Islamic intellectuals was responsible for the renewal of both philosophy and science in the Middle Ages. Without this renewal and renaissance in the twelfth century and thirteenth centuries, the Scientific Revolution in the sixteenth and seventeenth centuries in the West would have been impossible.

---

1 The Qu'ran is also commonly spelled Koran but Qu'ran is closer to the Arabic transliteration. According to *Webster's Third International Dictionary*, (1981), the Qu'ran is: "The book composed of writings accepted by Muslims as revelation made to Mohammed by Allah and as the divinely authorized basis for the religious, social, civil, commercial, military and legal regulations of the Islamic world."

2 Albert Einstein, *Out of My Later Years* (NY: Philosophical Library, 1950), 2.

3 Ibid., 26.

Introduction

The Scientific Revolution

The Scientific Revolution of the sixteenth and seventeenth centuries separated the natural sciences from the Aristotelian philosophical context that had endured for nearly 2000 years in Western civilization. In doing so, it opened the scientific enterprise to many wonder-filled scientific and technological discoveries and developments. It would, however, encase the philosophy of science into a reductionistic and mechanistic framework that deprived nature of her wonder and deepest meaning.

The contemporary understanding of man's place in nature within the Western world has evolved largely through a scientific understanding of humans as the central actors in command of nature and her riches. The exploration and exploitation of nature has allowed Western culture to achieve great accomplishments in physics, chemistry, biology, medicine and space science over the past 500 years. It has also brought about an ecological and spiritual crisis that threatens the existence of all forms of life on planet Earth. The threat of nuclear and biological warfare, known as weapons of mass destruction (WMD), is an ever-present barrier to world peace and has recently been used as a rationale and justification for the war against the nation of Iraq by the United

States. Many scientists assert that greenhouse gases are contributing to global warming and that this could bring about multiple changes in world weather patterns.[1] Such changes could lead to the loss of major portions of the earth's landmass because of melting polar ice caps.[2] The United Nations Framework Convention of Climate Change (UNFCCC) states the definition of climate change is a "change of climate which is attributed directly or indirectly to human activity that alters the composition of the global atmosphere and which is in addition to natural climate variability observed over comparable time periods."[3] Given the above definition of "climate change," global warming can have a profound impact on sea levels and affect future food production. "The problem with continued global warming is that it will cause the polar ice caps to melt, resulting in a rise in sea levels and consequent flooding of low-lying land, which could include whole countries (such as Bangladesh) and many world capital cities. A change in the climate would also affect crop growth."[4]

Continued loss of wetlands, forests and agricultural regions to various types of commercial and recreational development threaten the ecological balance that has sustained biodiversity for millions of years. It is this biodiversity that has formed the foundation for the emergence of *homo sapiens* and the birth of human civilization. The social and spiritual questions prompted by this growing ecological challenge have been well-documented by environmental studies. Various fast-growing environmental organizations such as the Sierra Club, Greenpeace and the Environmental Defense Fund seek to challenge the dominant paradigm of global, free-market capitalism and the *laissez-faire* economic assumptions that underlie it. The field of environmental and developmental ethics has become an important feature of the growing emphasis upon sustainable economic and ecological strategies for the twenty-first century.

The World Council of Churches, beginning in 1972 at the Stockholm meeting on the environment and a 1974 conference on "Science and Technology for Human Development: The Ambiguous Future—The Christian Hope," provided a dramatic critique of the economic philosophy of development that characterized much of the Western world in its relationship with poorer nations through most of the twentieth century.

> Global development as the "self-evident organizing principle of modern society" bore a materialism and secularism that undermined and destroyed traditional ways and worldviews. Mass-oriented consumption and communication undercut diversity and its values as a creational good. Technical rationality and consumption as a way of life were not advances and progress at all, but forces that disdained local culture, work, technology, lifestyle, religion, philosophy, mores and social institutions. Ancient religious and cultural practices were rendered quaint, and age-old questions of ultimate meaning and purpose were not considered significant matters of attention for "development." Spiritual vacuousness and homelessness set in, as did estrangement from the sacred and alienation from the earth.[5]

The Seventh Assembly of the World Council of Churches held in Canberra, Australia in 1991 had as its theme the renewal of the earth. The theme of the assembly was: "Come, Holy Spirit, Renew the Whole Creation." The assembly largely rejected the "dominion theology" (man's dominion over nature) that characterized much of Western religious thought over the past centuries of Western hegemony over world affairs and over nature. Francis Bacon's *Great Instauration* reflected these views in the statement which looks to the "enlarging of the bounds of human empire," by using nature as the "anvil" on which humans "hammer out" a world.[6] The comments of the noted historian, Lynn White, Jr., place the "imperialistic" comments of Bacon in a wider context: "The emergence in widespread practice of the Baconian creed that scientific knowledge means technological power over nature can scarcely be dated before about 1850, save in the chemical industries, where it is anticipated in the eighteenth century. Its acceptance as a normal pattern of action may mark the greatest event in human history since the invention of agriculture, and perhaps in nonhuman terrestrial history as well."[7] According to White, the West's fundamental attitude toward nature came from the Christian doctrine of creation that substituted a linear concept of time for the cyclical concept that dominated all previous cultures. White claims that Saint Francis put forth an alternative view of nature in the thirteenth century but that it never became the orthodox view of the West.

> The greatest spiritual revolutionary in Western history, Saint Francis, proposed what he thought was an alternative Christian view of nature and man's relation to it; he tried to substitute the idea of the equality of all creatures, including man, for the idea of man's limitless rule of creation. He failed. Both our present science and our present technology are so tinctured with orthodox Christian arrogance toward nature that no solution for our ecologic crisis can be expected from them alone. Since the roots of our trouble are so largely religious, the remedy must also be essentially religious, whether we call it that or not. We must rethink and renew our nature and destiny. The profoundly religious, but heretical, sense of the primitive Franciscans for the spiritual autonomy of all parts of nature may point a direction. I propose Francis as a patron saint for ecologists.[8]

Following White's assertion that the "orthodox Christian arrogance toward nature" cannot be expected to provide a solution to the ecological crisis, many in the environmental movement have turned toward eastern religious philosophies, such as Buddhism and Taoism, for inspiration. Other Christian theologians such as Thomas Berry and Brian Swimme have fashioned a new cosmology around the divine presence in nature. As Berry states, "Because our sense of the divine is so extensively derived from verbal sources, mostly from the biblical Scriptures, we seldom notice how much we have lost contact with the revelation of the divine in nature. Yet our exalted sense of the divine comes from the grandeur of the universe, especially from the earth in all the splendid modes of its expression."[9]

The Canberra meeting of the World Council of Churches held out a similar view of the sacredness of nature as understood within the Orthodox tradition of Christianity. This view is sometimes called "panentheism" because "it recognizes and celebrates the divine in, with and under all nature, ourselves included....To identify something earthly as holy and sacred is not to say it *is* God. Rather it is *of* God, God is present in its presence."[10]

An ecofeminist critique of traditional forms of patriarchal Christianity found in the Roman Catholic, Orthodox and Anglican communions "is that the sacramentalism of these traditions has served to reinforce powerful linkages of patriarchy, social domination and environmental degradation."[11] Rosemary Ruether, a noted feminist scholar and theologian, calls for a new "biophilic mutuality that cuts across not only gender, class and race, but also species lines."[12] Ruether's "biophilic mutuality" claims that the divine imprint is found both within human nature and all of creation. Patriarchy, according to Ruether, arose with "new human developments of control over food supply. Slavery, hierarchy, sexism, the treatment of land and animals as property all developed as aspects of a system of society called patriarchy."[13] Ruether believes that we are at a crossroads in the history of the planet and that "we are at a terminal stage of these patterns of patriarchal exploitation, a stage at which we either choose to learn new ways of relating that recapture biophilic mutuality on a new, consciously chosen, level, or else we will destroy ourselves and much of the life forms of the earth with us."[14]

The scientific community, in "An Open Letter to the Religious Community" dated January 1990 and written by 34 internationally renowned scientists led by Carl Sagan and Hans Bethe, called upon the religious community to address the environmental crisis the world is now facing. This letter described many aspects of environmental degradation and urged religious leaders to do their part in addressing these problems.

> Problems of such magnitude and solutions demanding so broad a perspective must be recognized from the outset as having a religious as well as scientific dimension. Mindful of our common responsibility, we scientists—many of us long engaged in combating the environmental crisis—urgently appeal to the world religious community to commit, in word and deed, and as boldly as required, to preserve the environment of the earth….Efforts to safeguard and cherish the environment need to be infused with vision of the sacred.[15]

The catastrophe of 9/11 in New York, Washington and Pennsylvania, and the recent (July, 2005) bombings in London have brought out how fragile the dominant Western culture is and how a few dedicated terrorists can bring death and destruction to the technologically-advanced civilization of the West. Billions of dollars are now spent on the new "crusade" against terrorists. The spiritual core of this crisis is, however, relegated to sound bites and disinformation about the true nature of this split between the materialism of the West and of indigenous and traditional societies. The spiritual or metaphysical issues that are raised may be of greater importance to the future of the human race than the latest scientific or technological advancements. The noted Islamic philosopher of science and spirituality, Seyyed Hossein Nasr, has stated the spiritual crisis in this way:

> Few are willing to look reality in the face and accept the fact that peace is not possible in human society as long as the attitude toward nature and the whole natural environment is one based on aggression and war. Furthermore, perhaps not all realize that in order to gain this peace with nature there must be peace with the spiritual order. To be at peace with the Earth one must

be at peace with Heaven....To remedy this situation the metaphysical knowledge pertaining to nature must be revived and the sacred quality of nature given back to it once again. In order to accomplish this end, the history and philosophy of science must be reinvestigated in relation to Christian theology and the traditional philosophy of nature that existed during most of European history....The result would be the bestowal once again of a sacred quality upon nature, providing a new background for the sciences without negating their value or legitimacy within their own domain."[16]

The sacred quality of nature is often best expressed in poetry, such as "God's Grandeur" by the noted nineteenth century Jesuit poet, Gerard Manley Hopkins

God's Grandeur
The world is charged with the grandeur of God
It will flame out, like shining from shook foil,
It gathers to greatness, like the ooze of oil
Crushed. Why do men then now not reck his rod?
Generations have trod, have trod, have trod;
And all is seared with trade, bleared, smeared with toil,
And wears man's smudge and shares man's smell:
the soil is bare now, nor can foot feel, being shod.
And for all this, nature is never spent;
There lives the dearest freshness, deep down things,
And though the last lights off the black West went
Oh, morning, at the brown brink eastward, springs –
Because the Holy Ghost over the bent
World broods with warm breast and with ah! Bright wings.[17]

Another approach to the contemporary spiritual crisis of Western culture is present in the Buddhist teachings of the Dalai Lama. In a recent editorial in the *New York Times*, the Dalai Lama notes that "disturbing emotions like anger, fear and hatred are giving rise to devastating problems throughout the world....But reflection shows that in our lives much of our suffering is caused not by external causes but by such events as the arising of disturbing emotions."[18] The Dalai Lama goes on to show the connection between spirituality and science by explaining how Western science is beginning to provide experimental evidence that "mindfulness" and "meditation" can transform these "disturbing emotions" or inoculate the practitioner against such emotional states. The Dalai Lama states that a neuroscientist, Dr. Richard Davidson at the University of Wisconsin, has used imaging devices to study the effects of Buddhist meditation. His research indicates that this type of meditation seems to "strengthen the neurological circuits that calm a part of the brain that acts as trigger for fear and anger."[19]

Similar experiments by Dr. Paul Ekman of the University of California at San Francisco indicate that a jarring noise, such as a gunshot, did not disturb the inner tranquility of a highly-trained meditation practitioner. Mindfulness meditation and other forms of contemplative spiritual practice, such as those found among Buddhist and Christian monks, may be the keys to transforming the Western dualism of man and nature. Spiritual tranquility brings us much closer to the interior dimension of nature that seems to be part of the ancient wisdom that we wish now to explore in this study.

Greek philosophical influences were largely centered upon the writings of Plato and Aristotle, the Athenian philosophers of the fifth and fourth centuries BCE. In addition to the emphasis of Greek philosophy upon the rational, the healing and medical traditions of ancient Greece provide us with insights on how the realms of spirituality and science were often viewed as complementary in the ancient world. The mythological and cosmological perspectives of ancient Greece and the Hellenistic era provided the popular culture of the ancient world with an integrated understanding of the physical and spiritual realms whereas Greek philosophy approached metaphysics through a more rational and logically-constrained mode of inquiry. Neither mode of inquiry was considered exclusive of the other in the ancient world.

This metaphysical and cosmological wisdom of antiquity passed into Islamic civilization in the early Middle Ages and was transformed by Islamic philosophers, scientists and mystics. In the West, a renewal of the ancient Hellenistic tradition occurred during the twelfth and thirteenth centuries with the translation of many philosophical and scientific works from the Islamic corpus into Latin. Over the next three centuries the foundation was laid for the Scientific Revolution of the sixteenth and seventeenth centuries as scholars studied these texts and refined the questions that they posed. The central question of man's relationship with nature is a unifying theme that evolved throughout this historical development. In the ancient and medieval world, physics (the present domain of contemporary science) and metaphysics (now the domain only of philosophy and religion in the West) were generally interdependent. The Scientific Revolution separated the natural sciences from the Aristotelian philosophical context that had endured for nearly 2000 years in western civilization. In doing so, it opened the scientific enterprise to many wonder-filled scientific and technological discoveries and developments. However, it would also encase the philosophy of science into a reductionistic and mechanistic framework that deprived nature of her wonder and deepest meaning. A key purpose of our study is to introduce students of both Western spirituality and science to the key insights that the Greek, Judeo-Christian and Islamic cultures brought to the discussion of nature and our place as human beings in nature. Within the ancient and medieval worldview, mythology and cosmology both were integral to the philosophy of science and the exploration of the natural world. Ancient and medieval cultures presumed that the myths which informed their thought processes were just as real as any scientific fact or rational explanation of a natural process. It is our understanding that each of these three streams of thought and culture—Greek, Judeo-Christian and Muslim—played somewhat equal roles in the formation of the Western scientific culture that began to emerge in the late Middle Ages. Without this preparatory period of textual transmission, scholastic methodology and university-based education and research, the Scientific Revolution hardly seems possible. The noted historian of medieval and early modern science, Edward Grant, has stated this case very well.

> My attitude changed dramatically, however, when, some years ago, I asked myself whether a Scientific Revolution could have occurred in the seventeenth century if the level of science in Western Europe had remained what it was in the first half of the twelfth century. That is, could a scientific revolution have occurred in the seventeenth century if the massive translations of Greco-Arabic science and natural philosophy into Latin had never taken place? The response seemed obvious: no, it could not. Without the translations, many centuries would have been required before Western Europe could have reached the level of Greco-Arabic science, thus delaying any possibility of a transformation of science. But the translations did occur and so did the Scientific Revolution. It follows that something happened between approximately 1200 and 1600 that proved conducive for the production of a Scientific Revolution.[20]

It is our purpose to help place the momentous event of the transmission of Greco-Arabic science and natural philosophy into its broader historical context as part of the legacy of Western civilization. In his latest book, noted historian of the Middle East, Professor Richard Bulliet of Columbia University, argues forcefully that we should refer to Western civilization as the "Islamo-Christian Civilization." His book shows the continuing interdependence of these two cultures over the past one thousand years and their continuing need to understand each other as siblings rather than as enemies. "The past and future of the West cannot be fully comprehended without appreciation of the twinned relationship it has had with Islam over some fourteen centuries. The same is true of the Islamic world."[21]

We hope the reader will better understand the intellectual foundations for our Western scientific culture after they have read our study of its origins in the Greek, Christian and Islamic cultures that preceded it. The Tsunami catastrophe of December, 2004 reminds us that the earth cannot be completely controlled or manipulated for human purposes. The rise of human civilization must be placed within a larger cosmic framework that requires a philosophical and spiritual context which lies beyond the traditional boundaries of experimental science. We will now explore the meaning of the concept of "science" as it evolved within the ancient and medieval worldview in Greek, Islamic and Christian contexts. In an earlier period of history, "science" was not limited to the modern scientific method of observation, experimentation, verification and validation. It encompassed multiple bodies of knowledge that were organized in a hierarchical fashion with philosophy and theology standing at its apex.

---

[1] For the latest scientific evidence about global warming, see the *New Scientist* web site: http://www.newscientist.com/channel/earth/climate-change/ (accessed July 28, 2005).

[2] See "Global Warming puts the Arctic on Thin Ice," National Resources Defense Council report. http://www.nrdc.org/globalWarming/qthinice.asap (accessed 7-28-05).

[3] U.S. Environmental Protection Agency, U.S. Greenhouse Gas Inventory Program, "Greenhouse Gases and Global Warming Potential Values," April, 2003, p. 3. www.epa.gov/globalwarming/publications/emissions

[4] Percy Harrison and Gillian Waites, eds., *The Cassell Dictionary of Science* (London: Cassell, 1997), 188. For a discussion of the growing awareness of the need to address global climate change within the international business community, see the lead article by John Carey, "Global Warming" in *Business Week* (New York: McGraw Hill, August 16, 2004), 62. Remarkably, business is far ahead of Congress and the White House. Some CEOs are already calling for once-unthinkable steps. "We accept that the science on global warming is overwhelming," says John W. Rowe, chairman and CEO of Exelon Corp. "There should be mandatory carbon constraints." For the lastest information on climate change see the study of the <u>Intergovermental Report on Climate Change</u>, winner of the 2007 Nobel Peace Prize: www.ipcc.com

[5] Larry L. Rasmussen, *Earth Community, Earth Ethics* (Maryknoll, NY: Orbis Books, 1998), 140.

[6] Ibid., 230.

[7] White, Lynn JrLynn White, Jr., "The Historical Roots of Our Ecological Crisis," *Science*, vol. 155, (10 March 1967), 1203.

[8] Ibid., 1207.

[9] Anne Lonergan and Caroline Richards, eds., *Thomas Berry and the New Cosmology* (Mystic, CT: Twenty-Third Publications, 1990), 17.

[10] Rasmussen, *Earth Community, Earth Ethics*, 239.

[11] Rasmussen, *Earth Community, Earth Ethics*, 239.

[12] Rosemary Radford Reuther, *Women and Redemption: A Theological History* (Minneapolis: Fortress Press, 1998), 223.

[13] Ibid., 223.

[14] Ibid., 224.

[15] Rasmussen, *Earth Community, Earth Ethics*, 183.

[16] Seyyed Hossein Nasr, *Man and Nature: The Spiritual Crisis in Modern Man* (Chicago: ABC International Group, 1997), 13 – 14.

[17] Gerard Manley Hopkins, "God's Grandeur." Full text and commentary may be found at www.bartleby.com/1227.html.

[18] Dalai Lama, New York Times, April 26, 2003, Op Ed page, www.nytimes.com/2003/04/26LAMA.html

[19] Ibid.

[20] Edward Grant, *The Foundations of Modern Science in the Middle Ages: Their Religious, Institutional and Intellectual Context* (Cambridge, UK: Cambridge University Press, 1996), xiii.

[21] Richard Bulliet, *The Case for Islamo-Christian Civilization* (New York: Columbia University Press, 2004).

Chapter One

Meaning of the Concept of Science

In this pragmatic sense, science has constantly evolved over the centuries and helped humanity to evolve with it. Science has not had a single meaning over the centuries but its meaning has tended to be a function of the purpose that it served in ancient, medieval and modern societies.

Today, the word "science" is very familiar to us. It is the magic word of modern life, and almost all material amenities of life flow from science and technology. Science is the necessary handmaiden of technology and economic progress in the modern world. Scientific inventions are at the root of technology. Technology produces goods and facilities for the comfort and enjoyment of life. Modern life revolves around science and technology particularly in the economies of the Western world.[1]

In the view of one of the greatest thinkers of the Orient, Abu Nasr al-Farabi (870 – 950 CE),[2] the foremost requirement of the human race is the survival and development of human life. In our challenging and competitive global world, science and technology have become central to a more humane life. Science and technology are indispensable in all spheres of human activity:

individual, familial social, political, economic, religious, diplomatic. Science has largely become the dominant paradigm for understanding man's place in the universe, including the exploration of our solar system and beyond.[3]

From its earlier subservient position as handmaiden to theology, science has assumed an indifferent or threatening posture toward morality and religion. In the ancient world, religion and morality mutually aided each other in enthroning Divine Providence as the crowning principle of human life.[4] In the modern world, a kind of scientific-logical imperative of self-reliance resides in many sectors and cultures. This has loosened the bond of Divine Providence. As a result, a strain of enlightenment secularism[5] is prevalent everywhere, making science and purely rational thought the dominant influences in Western society. Science and technology are now considered the principal barometers of economic progress. All nations are vying with one another to build up academic facilities of basic science and institutional facilities of low and high technology. Moreover, in the current ultra-modern nuclear age, technology has grown to amazing proportions. High technology is guiding the steps of the fastest-growing human civilizations, wherein technologically advanced nations like the United States, Japan, and the nations of Europe are relentlessly struggling to surpass one another. Novel scientific inventions and innovative technological devices are the front lines of the prosperity of nations.

Development of technology depends upon innovations in basic science. In a world engulfed by nationalistic jealousies, the virtues and vices of nationalism are keeping nations at arms length and forcing them into global competition for new technologies. Hence, the more developed a nation is in basic sciences and high technology, the more advanced it is in the scale of prosperity and culture. Such nations are presently playing crucial roles in the field of economic development and in the affairs of the United Nations. In this pragmatic sense, science has constantly evolved over the centuries and humanity has evolved with it. Historically, science has not had a single meaning over the centuries; its meaning has tended to be a function of the purpose that it served. In the present age, it has tended to become synonymous with advancement, modernism, progress and prosperity. It is hoped that the Muslim world can revive the modern notion of science and show that it, too, can evolve into a meaningful construct for contemporary Islamic cultures. Muslim culture is moving toward an integration of contemporary science and technology within its own cultural context. It is, therefore, imperative that we explore the meaning of "science" within the historic Islamic culture and its relationship to the Christian philosophy of science in the Middle Ages.

In the investigation of "science" in Islamic culture, we are prone to believe that "science," as an original Arabic word, *al-ulum at-tajribiyah*, was a translation of the phrase "experimental sciences." On closer scrutiny, however, we find that this word and the concept behind it need further clarification.

The Root of Science

In Latin, *scio* is said to mean "to know in the widest sense or significance of the word, that is, to understand, to perceive, to have knowledge of or skill in anything whatsoever." It is also said that *scio* means to ordain, decree or appoint anything after the requisite knowledge is obtained regarding it. The infinitive form of *scio* is *scire*[6] which means to understand and to know. In its most general sense, "science" usually meant an organized body of knowledge, and was considered a part of natural philosophy in the ancient and medieval world.

The *World University Encyclopedia* derives the word "science" from the same Latin root of *scire*, meaning to know, and confirms the meaning of science as "any form of organized knowledge."[7] For instance, the linguistic history of "science" implies: "The state or facts of knowing, knowledge or cognizance of something specified or implied; not only in theology, in the sense of knowledge but as opposed to belief or opinion." Perceptual knowledge or sense knowledge was often considered unreliable in the ancient world because of the changing character of sense impressions. Plato and the Neoplatonists[8] who followed him in this tradition were particularly mistrustful of the reliability of sense knowledge. The Neoplatonists developed theories of illumination, which seemed to make any reliable, rational knowledge dependent upon some form of direct contact with an immaterial form of knowledge that emanated from the divine source (often called the *One* in Neoplatonic thought). In the Neoplatonic tradition, this "form" was usually known as *Nous* or Reason. It was the source of intelligibility for any empirical knowledge. Neoplatonic theories of illumination were, then, a kind of inspirational knowledge and, as we shall see, this was the intellectual foundation for much of the Oxford Augustinian School of philosophy in the thirteenth century. Even "reason" itself was rooted in some form of supra-sensible knowledge that was common to both the Islamic and Christian epistemology of that era. Knowledge of revelation in both the Christian and Islamic tradition was based upon a theory of divine authority underlying the written Word of God in the Hebrew and Christian Scriptures and the Islamic Qu'ran. Commentaries on the Scriptures and the Qu'ran were considered to have a different level of authority than the directly-inspired revelation given to the authors of these sacred books. From 1340 to 1728, therefore, the word "science" was not used in a strictly scientific sense to mean experimental objective knowledge, but in an analogous sense regarding symbolic or mysterious knowledge pertaining either to the mystery of Nature or a sign of God. These views equate the English word "science" with the Latin word *scientia*. In addition, "science" stands as an equivalent for the Arabic-Hebrew word *ayah* or *ayat*, which means the sign of the process of creation or the mystery of creation.

Thus, the use of the word "science," whether stemming from *scientia* or *scire*, is quite distinct from the meaning and implication of "modern science." "Modern science" offers us an objective knowledge of "phenomena" derived through observation, verification and experiment, whereas the knowledge commonly spoken of in Islam and Christianity in the Middle Ages is knowledge of the *noumena* or metaphysical world. This is a thoroughly intuitive, imaginative, and speculative process, yet it also is rooted in centuries of human wisdom passed down to us from the Greco-Roman, Islamic and Christian cultures.

The *Oxford Dictionary* draws a distinction between science and art in the Greek usage. It says that, distinguished from art, a science is concerned with theoretical truth; art, with methods for effecting certain results. Sometimes, however, the term "science" is extended to denote a body of practical knowledge, which depends on the understanding and conscious application of principles. Art, on the other hand, is understood to require merely knowledge of traditional rules and skill acquired by repetition.[9]

It is clear, then, that "natural philosophy" stood in for "natural science" or "experimental science" until the nineteenth century.[10] By that time, the significance of the word "science" shifted to mean a demonstrated body of knowledge brought about through deductive reasoning. John F. Herschel, an originator of the scientific analytical methodology, wrote *Preliminary Discourse on the Study of Natural Philosophy*, published in London in 1830.[11] The word "science," in its contemporary usage, did not come into common currency in Greek, Latin or any other European languages until after the publication of Herschel's work.

We do know, however, that the *Académie des Sciences* was formed in Paris during the seventeenth century and that "science" could be considered part of the agenda of Enlightenment. The Enlightenment attempted to develop a naturalistic theory of knowledge that was not dependent upon any metaphysical or theological rationale for its understanding of the natural world.

The question regarding the derivation of the word "science" remains. Why the term *scientia*? Did it originally have a broader meaning than it does today?

Analysis from Historical Perspectives

The term *scientia* points to the historically significant fact that this word was also a technical term, and was often linked to an adjunct, for example, "experimental science." These special traits take us back to the thirteenth century when the great Christian theological reformer-scientist Roger Bacon wrote his masterpiece *Opus Majus*. In this monumental book, he used the term *scientia experimentalis* for the first time, presumably as an equivalent of the popularly current Arabic terminology *al-ulum at-tajribiyah*. Thus, *scientia* probably stood for *ulum* in the generic sense of "knowledge" and *experimentalis* stood for *tajribiyah*. (Bacon does not use the term *scientia* in the plural usage, *scientiae*, but only in the singular). Because "experimental science" is the foundation of modern science, without *experimentalis*, science or *scientia*, it would have no place in the modern world. Contemporary scholarship questions whether Bacon really meant an "experimental method" in the modern sense of the term.[12] Bacon was more concerned with *observation* than with *demonstration* in his *Opus Majus*. He did, however, have an interest in the science of optics and is credited with the invention of spectacles. His writings on optics seemed to complement his Augustinian philosophical orientation with its emphasis on light and a theory of illumination that governed his understanding of this topic.

Augustine held that all knowledge was meant to draw us into the contemplation of an infinite and eternal object of knowledge, namely God. According to Augustine's theory, only knowledge of God can bring happiness to the soul. Knowledge, then, is a kind of wisdom of the heart and soul and not just the abstract knowledge of the mind. Plato had suggested a theory of reminiscence to explain how the soul could know eternal and immutable truths since sense knowledge was considered transitory and impermanent. Augustine, with some similarity to Descartes, held that we do have a certain knowledge of reality even if our sense knowledge is imperfect. We know that we exist and that we are able to understand the world in which we live. All this is known by our inner experience of self-awareness and self-consciousness. Sense knowledge, for Augustine, was known "through" or "in the light of" the soul, that is, "knowledge does not come from the body but from the soul through the body."[13]

The rational soul, according to Augustine, is the source of true knowledge and can grasp eternal truth even though sense impressions may be skewed. The rational soul, in effect, uses the sense organs for access to the sensible world but the interior world of the soul transcends all sense knowledge and gives a person access to eternal and divine truth. Therefore, the lowest level of knowledge is sensation, and the highest level of knowledge is contemplation of the divine and eternal realm of being. The soul can direct its intellect and will toward practical pursuits that lead to experiential truths, but these are of a different order than those learned through contemplation of eternal truths. Eternal truths are available to all. Mathematics seemed closer to the realm of eternal truth because it acted as a bridge between the worlds of sensible knowledge and eternal knowledge.

Augustine also held that the eternal truths were similar to the Platonic Forms or Ideas but they were, in his epistemology, rooted ontologically in the mind of God and accessible only to the human mind through some form of "divine illumination." The theory of illumination served as kind of conduit between the human soul and the "mind" of God. In this way, the human soul would not directly "know" the mind of God but would "know" in the light of divine action to enlighten the human mind. In the Neoplatonic concept of light, the divine light radiates down into the world of materiality from the spiritual world of pure light. Similar to Plotinus, God or the One emanates divine rays down through the various celestial spheres into the material and corporeal realm. In his *De Trinitate*, Augustine states that the nature of the mind is such that "when directed to intelligible things in the natural order, according to the disposition of the Creator, it sees them in a certain incorporeal light which is *sui generic* (unique) just as the corporeal eye sees adjacent objects in the corporeal light."[14]

We can see, then, that for Augustine and his followers such as Roger Bacon the "science" of light was crucial for his epistemology on both the levels of knowledge of Nature and knowledge of God. Spiritual illumination performed the same function for the soul as sunlight did for the human eye. Sight functioned for the eye as the vehicle for recognizing the exemplary ideas that resided ultimately in the mind of God. These two types of illumination were analogous to one another and provided a metaphysical foundation for the science of optics, which Bacon and his Islamic predecessors undertook. They viewed this science as ultimately rooted in the form of divine illumination, which allowed the human mind to view the truth. In the medieval worldview, the natural sciences and divine science were inextricably interwoven. Regarding the Latin *scientia*, another interesting point takes us one century earlier. During the tenth century, during the Abbasid Caliphate, Abu Nasr al-Farabi, the great Muslim philosopher, was regarded as the most revered teacher after Aristotle and wrote a book entitled *Isha' al-Ulum* (*Enumeration of Science*). In the twelfth century, it was partly translated into Latin by the famous Orientalist, Dominican Gundisalvi and partly by another great Orientalist, Gerard of Cremona, who completed it in 1175. Both works were entitled *De Scientiis*.[15] Gundisalvi and Gerard were theologians and both must have translated the word *scientii* for *sulum*, ("sciences") from the Latin root words *scientia* (*scientiis* is the plural form of *De Scientiis*, "Concerning the Sciences.") Hence, significant historical evidence implies that another Latin expression was used to express the plurality of the "sciences" and clarifies the word *scientia*.

The Common Phrase: Experimental Sciences

The version of the Latin dictionary that asserts "science" has been derived from *scientia* is roughly, if not literally, corroborated by Gundisalvi's and Gerard's translation of *ulum* into *scientiis*. The Arabic word *ulum* is the plural of *ilm*, which, in turn, is derived form *alam*. *Alam* means a sign or symbol by means of which a thing is identified. *Ilm* stands for an academic discipline or a science. Thus, "sign" in English stands for *alam* in Arabic and "science" for *ilm*. However, in the Arabic usage, "science" is often dealt with in plural since a single scientific discipline does not give complete knowledge. Hence, science is always thought of as a totality, such as *al-'ulum at-siyassiyah* (political sciences), *al-'ulum al-tab'iyat* (natural sciences), *al-ulum al-tajribiyah* (experimental sciences), *al-ulum al-diniyah* (religious sciences.) Gundisalvi's *scientiis* was meant to be the translation of the plural word *ulum*; hence the suffix "s" may have stood for the plural of *scientia*. Moreover, if "science" is regarded as the equivalent of *ilm* through a common meaning contained in English words, signs or symbols, then all symbolic knowledge can potentially be considered the object of research. A particular kind of knowledge, designated in Arabic as *tajribiyah*, is equivalent to what Roger Bacon called "experimental knowledge" or *scientia experimentalis*. This implies that scientific knowledge is more than just an abstract universal concept as Aristotle had claimed.

But looking at the elegance of the repeated use of "Science of God" by the Christian theologians and poets, the simple meaning of "science" as a sign, symbol of, or pointer to, the mystery of the creation of God, suggests itself. In that case, *scientia*, "science," and "sign" stand equivalent to Arabic *alam*, the signing object itself, rather than *ilm*, the conceptual knowledge of the object. Therefore, we accept *scientiis* and *scientia* as translations of *ilm* and *ulum*. The term "science," then, stands on par with *alam* or sign or symbol of a thing, rendered *ayat* in the religious vocabulary of Arabic. We should see that the complementary relationship between the various types of knowledge described by medieval philosophers as a possible model (rather than paradigm) for the modern age. This model would respect the integrity of each discipline yet see that that they spring from the same ultimate source and are only understood by human beings who share similar world views.

This extensive analysis of these Arabic and Latin words does not prove that one is the exact correlative of the other; rather, they show that there were similar meanings for the Arabic and Latin words dealing with similar concepts. We know that, in some cases, the Latin was a rough translation of Arabic terms. Nor can we imply that Bacon had in mind the same cultural equivalent of the Arabic words since they had a cultural context distinct from each other at this time. It does seem probable, however, that given the Neoplatonic orientation of Bacon, all knowledge would be considered "godly" because it was illumined by the same divine sources, whether purely conceptual or experiential. Both the Qu'ran and the Hebrew and Christian Scriptures teach that all human knowledge can be seen as a sign or symbol leading to divine knowledge. The Qu'ranic term *ayat* or *alam* can be translated into English as "science," yet it also infers that this knowledge is a sign leading one to the Godhead. The closest word we have to *ayat* in English would probably be the word "wisdom." The Hebrew Book of Wisdom is filled with practical and "experiential" knowledge that leads to the path of righteousness and union with God. The sacred scriptures of the three great monotheistic faiths reflect a view that sees all of creation as transparent to the divine presence but mediated through the created natural order which reflects the intent and design of the creator. The medieval Christian philosophers and theologians of the thirteenth and fourteenth centuries began to use the term *scientia experimentalis* in some of their writings. Robert Grosseteste, Roger Bacon and William of Ockham were three of the key interpreters of a method that would be called *via moderna* (modern way) by the beginning of the fourteenth century. They still held to the basic tenets of Aristotelian logic, which emphasized deductive methods of demonstration. However, they began to explore mathematical methods that verified their deductive conclusions. They also relied on experiential knowledge for other forms of verification because, by the time of Ockham, they had rejected the extra-mental reality of universals. If only individual things were actually and objectively real, it would necessitate more emphasis on attention to the empirical basis for human knowing. The followers of the *via moderna*, however, did not use an inductive and experimental method of observation with rigorous methods of proof. Their understanding of "experimental" was much more related to validation of their mathematical conclusions by methods of approximation rather than by strict demonstration.

By the time of Galileo and Descartes, a much more inductive method of demonstration began to arise. This inductive method was "canonized" as a tool of modernity by Francis Bacon in his *Novum Organon* of 1620. The use of the term *scientia experimentalis* in the nineteenth century took on another meaning, which was influenced by the mechanistic and atomistic world that was systematically defined by Descartes (1596 – 1650). Galileo had discovered new facts about the natural world through his experimental methods, which were governed by mathematical laws. Descartes took Galileo's insights and utilized their implications to develop a rigorous philosophy of nature based upon mathematical physics.

Descartes' philosophy of nature applied mathematics to natural phenomena. For Descartes, *scientia experimentali*s meant the discovery of the mathematical laws that he knew through empirical methods. Such mathematical laws in the view of Descartes governed the entire physical universe. He rejected the Aristotelian methods of syllogistic demonstration in favor of a mathematical method. All of physical reality, for Descartes, revolved around matter and motion. He could, therefore, with the aid of mathematics, discover the mechanical laws which served as the intellectual structure for the universe. In the view of Descartes, the world and the soul are two distinct substances with almost nothing in common. Cartesian dualism is based upon his philosophy of substance. He held that the body is *res extensa* (a thing with physical extension), and that soul is *res cogitans* (a thinking substance). The body and mind dualism that we find in Descartes is often seen as the final dividing line between the medieval and modern world.[16]

The implications of this dualism for "experimental science" are noteworthy. The Cartesian understanding of the natural world separates mind and matter and the method of science is centered on the mind's discovery of objective mechanical laws that govern the natural world. The role of science is to discover these mechanical laws and demonstrate their accuracy through mathematical or geometric computations.

Philological and Historical Considerations of "Science"

The word "science" has undergone many changes of meaning over the past one thousand years. It was not until the nineteenth century that it assumed its present meaning connoting a demonstrable method of verification based upon observable methods of experimentation and testing of hypotheses. As an English word it is used in literature in 1340, 1426, 1601 and 1728, depicting symbolic knowledge as well as a theological foundation. However, in the present usage, it has completely lost its earlier connotation and has acquired only the meaning and implication of Bacon's *scientia experimentalis* (experimental knowledge). It may be recalled that Roger Bacon (1214 – 1492) first used the phrase *scientia experimentalis* in Latin in his famous work *Opus Majus*. The work was forwarded to Pope Clement in 1267. Recent scholarship questions the novelty of Bacon's phrase but it did imply that knowledge brought by "experience," in contrast to that which could only come from abstract principles such as those espoused by Aristotle in his writings on logic.

In *Opus Majus*, Bacon shifted the "object of scientific inquiry from the Aristotelian 'nature of forms' to laws of nature in a recognizable modern sense...."[17] Bacon felt that all experimental knowledge or *scientia experimentalis* was indebted to mathematics: "It is true indeed, that mathematics has universal experiences concerning its conclusions in figuring and numbering, which are applied likewise to all sciences and to this experimental science, because no science can be known without mathematics."[18] Until recently, Bacon's fame rested on his brief writings on experimental science. He was, however, also very interested in the science of optics. He drew much of his understanding of optics from the writings of two Muslim thinkers, Alhazen (Ibn al-Haitham: 965 – 1039) and Avicenna (Ibn Sina, 980 – 1037). Bacon's study of optics was connected to his interest in "experimental science" because it was by means of vision that "we search out certain experimental knowledge of all things that are in the heavens and in the earth."[19] Crombie states that "his account of vision was one of the most important written during the Middle Ages and it became a point of departure for seventeenth-century work. Bacon's chief contribution was to try to explain the operation of the eye, of which his account was based largely on the writings of Alhazen and Avicenna."[20] Ibn al-Haitham was one of the great Muslim physicists of the early medieval period. He wrote many manuscripts on mathematics, physics, astronomy and medicine. He resided in Cairo for much of his adult life and it was probably there that he wrote his most famous treatise on optics, *Opticae Thesaurus*. This Latin translation was probably done at the end of the twelfth century and certainly influenced Roger Bacon in his writing of the *Opus Majus*. The Latin translation may also have influenced later writers including Witelo and Kepler.[21] This treatise remained the standard optical textbook in Western Europe until the seventeenth century. It was, in fact, the greatest of all books on optics until Kepler. Even Kepler and Descartes used Ibn al-Haitham's experimental methods in their studies.[22] Bacon became especially interested in optics through a study of the Latin version of the works of al-Haitham. Through these works, Bacon understood mirrors and lenses and described the telescope. Part V of Bacon's *Opus Majus* is practically a copy of al-Haitham's optics.[23] Bacon also gave a theory of the rainbow as an example of inductive reasoning after studying the work of Ibn al-Haitham. To speak specifically of al-Haitham's contribution to optics, one is first reminded of his work on the eye. Before the time of al-Haitham, the established Greek theory of vision, according to Galen, Euclid and Ptolemy, was that light emanated from the beholder's eye and fell on the object, which then became visible. As is now known, this was entirely incorrect.

Ibn al-Haitham was the first scholar to offer an accurate theory of vision. He correctly deduced from experiments that light starts from the object we see and enters the eye wherein an image is formed and the object becomes visible. It is rather surprising to note that for hundreds of years (since Euclid's time) an incorrect theory of vision persisted among the Greeks and even among the astute Alexandrians in Egypt. In order to arrive at the correct theory of vision, al-Haitham performed a number of experiments and studied the composition of the eye by dissection. In his book, *Optical Thesaurus, (Kitab al-Manazir)* he discussed the anatomy and physiology of the eye. He traced the functioning of the eye from the optic nerve originating in the brain to the eye itself. He described the various parts, such as the conjunctiva, iris, cornea and lens, and pointed out the role of each. He also showed the interrelation between the various parts of the eye and how the eye acts as a unitary organ and as a refracting system during the process of vision. Avicenna (ibn Sina 980 – 1037) is often compared with Aristotle and is usually considered the greatest philosopher/scientist in Islamic intellectual history. Avicenna was a child prodigy who mastered all the major philosophical and scientific knowledge of his day. He spent most of his adult life in Persia where he was best known as a physician to the Buwayhid princes of Persia. He is still venerated in Persia and a memorial is located at his place of burial at Hamadan in modern-day Iran. His best known work was the *Canon of Medicine*, which was available to Bacon and many other medieval and renaissance philosophers and "scientists." It was one of the most quoted medical texts in medieval universities through the late middle ages and the Renaissance.[24] A contemporary historian of medieval English medicine, Faye Getz, states:

Scientific learning, of which medicine was a part, likewise was transformed by the West's discovery of Islamic scholarship. In England scholars like Adelard of Bath, Alfred of Sareschel, John Blund and the Jewish convert Petrus Alfonsi brought learning about the natural sciences from the European continent largely by means of translations from the Arabic.[25] According to Avicenna, the practice of medicine was

> ...divided into theory, practice and empiricism. Medical theory concerned truths that were axiomatic—that there were four humors, for instance—while practice concerned how these truths were put into operation.

Empiricism concerned knowledge that was gathered from experience alone, without learned justification."[26]

We can surmise that Bacon was familiar with Avicenna's concept of experimental knowledge because he refers to Avicenna in his treatise on pharmacology, *Antiodarium*.[27] Bacon held that both reason and experience should guide the dispensing of medicine. According to Crombie,

> ...the real founder of the tradition of scientific thought in medieval Oxford and, in some ways, of the modern English intellectual tradition was Roger Bacon. Grosseteste united in his own work the experimental and rational traditions of the twelfth century and set forth a systematic theory of experimental science.[28]

Grosseteste, according to a recent study by James McEvoy, made "a distinctive contribution to the University of Oxford, the earliest years of which (up to 1235) he may be fairly said to have dominated, intellectually speaking."[29] Again, Crombie states

> The writer who most thoroughly grasped, and who most elaborately developed Grosseteste's attitude to nature and theory of science was Roger Bacon (ca.1219 – 1292) himself. Recent research has shown that in many of the aspects of his science in which he has been thought to have been most original, Bacon was simply taking over the Oxford and Grosstestian tradition, though he was able also to make use of new sources unknown to Grosseteste, as, for example, the Optics of Alhazen (ibn al-Haitham).[30]

Both Grosseteste and Bacon were familiar with Avicenna's *Canon of Medicine* and with Avicenna's theories about the division of medical knowledge and his understanding of "scientific methods." It was not the scientific method of nineteenth-century England. It was, instead, the experiential knowledge brought about by careful observation and inquiry into the natural causes of events, particularly those which disrupted the natural flow of energies found in the body. With his theory of Augustinian divine illumination in mind, Bacon connected the theological mode of knowing and the natural, experiential mode governed by a theory of divine and human "sight."

We shall shortly return to the importance of the Augustinian and Neoplatonic theories of illumination for a full understanding of Bacon's thought and how he connected his understanding of the natural sciences with his theological reflection. We can hardly underestimate, however, his indebtedness to the intellectual heritage he received from Robert Grosseteste. In addition, Grosseteste's influence extended to the other great luminary of thirteenth century philosophy and medieval scientific thought, Albert the Great or Albertus Magnus (ca. 1206 – 1280). According to Crombie, "Albertus Magnus resembled Grosseteste in setting out a theory of experimental science in a commentary on the *Posterior Analytics* and, in fact, he used Grosseteste's commentary for this purpose."[31] It should be noted again that the "experimental science" of which Crombie speaks is really more an "experiential" knowledge of that time based upon a classification of nature still rooted in the Aristotelian categories of thought, namely, material, efficient and formal causes. It was not, however, a mere description of events but an analysis of the causes of those events that could be correlated into a systematic pattern. Albert the Great's studies on zoology, botany, geology and chemistry are well known and provide an insight into the "scientific method" of understanding the causes of natural phenomena and their resultant ordering within various branches of the natural sciences. Grosseteste's greatest influence upon Albert the Great seems to have been in Albert's study of meteorological optics.[32]

Crombie states that Bacon developed "perhaps the earliest explicit statement of the practical conceptions of the aims of science"[33] J. D. North, the eminent historian of science, takes exception to the views of Crombie and states that Bacon draws no clear line between systematic and purposeful experimentation and the accruing of experience. North also takes exception to Bacon's so-called incipient scientific method of verification by showing that he was heavily reliant on the authority of Islamic philosophy and science. Bacon, according to North, was also indebted to the Muslim philosopher scientist Al-Kindi in Bacon's work entitled *De multiplicacione specierum*.[34]

Bacon's reliance upon Muslim authorities may have been part of the reason for his censure by Church authorities near the end of his life. Bacon was greatly influenced by certain theories of magic rooted in his understanding of geometry and astronomy. He also had a certain distrust of the mythic Saracens, which seemed to contradict his reliance upon Islamic philosophy and natural sciences. This ambivalence within Bacon's thought was, however, part of the cultural fabric in which he lived. The Crusades also brought a highly suspicious attitude about the danger that the Saracens represented. All of these seemingly contradictory attitudes and views are expressed in the *Opus Majus*. As North states so well, "It is wrong to regard Roger Bacon as a simple prototype of the modern empirical scientist, but there is a case of sorts to be made for the idea, as long as we are prepared to leave a place for a belief in magical influence."[35] North does not dispute, however, the key role played by Islamic sources in the evolution of Bacon's understanding of the natural sciences. In his *Canon of Medicine*, Avicenna deals with physiology, aetiology, symptomatology and the principles of therapy. He also divides nature into three realms: the vegetable, animal and mineral domains. There are 800 chapters in the section dealing with the different herbs, their qualities, preparation of medicines and their strengths, effects and methods of use in treating different diseases. The names of the herbs are listed in alphabetical order in Arabic. In his discussion of pathology he includes symptoms, diagnosis and treatment of diseases of various parts of the body, including the head, chest, alimentary, excretory and genital systems. This book gives a picture of illnesses of the whole body, plus aspects of fever and its types and causes. In one chapter, he deals with poisonous vegetables, poisons of animal and mineral origin, poisoning due to animal bites, and their treatments. Another chapter deals with cosmetics, diseases of hair and nails, bad odor, and slim and obese bodies. He also provides the prescriptions for pills, powders, syrups, and extractions, along with their doses and methods of preparation.

Avicenna could also be considered one of the founders of psychotherapy for he was regarded as an innovator in the field of mental health and showed the connection between psychic states and physical health. He was the first to put forward the theory of brain localization, for he thought that the external senses, (sight, hearing, touch, taste, and smell) were centered in the brain. This has now been proven. Campbell claims that the _Canon of Medicine_ is the final codification of all Greco-Arabian medicine. It formed half the medical curriculum of European universities in the later part of the fifteenth century and continued as a textbook up to the middle of the seventeenth century in the universities of Montpellier and Louvain.[36] There were several translations of the _Canon_ in Greek, Latin and Hebrew rendered from 1079 to 1608. The Latin _Canon_ was printed 36 times in the fifteenth and the sixteenth centuries.[37] Avicenna was studied throughout the West and reached the Gaelic- speaking people of the British Islands as evidenced in the Scottish collection of Gaelic medical manuscripts.[38]

Grossteste referred to Avicenna by name in his _De Natura Locorum._ Grosstese and Avicenna held that the cause of an ailment could be understood either by _reasoning_ or by some method of _induction._ Roger Bacon, like Avicenna, was indebted to the method of earlier Arabic scientific writing.

> In medieval literature in general and particularly in the works of Roger Bacon we should handle the word "experiential" with care and be aware of attributing to it or to the word "experimentum"....As a rule "experiential" and "experimentum" do not have a much broader meaning than that of experience (or of something that we have acquired in this way), whenever and wherever

it may have been made. I now surmise that "scientia experimentalis" translates Alhazen's Arabic "al-itibar," which I have seen translated as "learning by example" and "instructive example" as well as "observation." Roger Bacon was a keen reader of Alhazen's works and some scholars claim (correctly I believe) that some of his key ideas come from there.[39]

Getz also points out that Bacon prepared a commentary on another famous medical text attributed to Aristotle called *Secretum Secretorum* that was

> ...actually the work of an unknown Islamic writer. The appeal of the *Secretum* was that is offered advice to the ultimate warrior prince on how to live well.... The *Secretum*...was not a university medical text, or even a Christian document; instead, it offered a textual approach for the philosophically trained to a royal or noble patron. Medical advice was not offered in isolation. It was rather integrated into more general advice on matters such as when to arise, what to eat, how to choose one's servants and the proper forms of dress and discourse.[40]

Bacon also wrote a treatise on the errors that prevailed among the physicians of his time called *De erroribus medicorum*. Both Grosseteste and Bacon shared similar concerns about incorporating the healing arts into the curriculum for a Christian education. They used the term *scientia experimentalis* to refer to the "practical arts" rather than to our contemporary understanding of a demonstrable scientific method involving verifiable testing and review by the scientific community. Nevertheless, this *scientia experimentalis* seems to have reflected a new emphasis on what we might today call "preventive medicine," dealing with the underlying causes of ill health and not just its symptoms.

From 1130 to 1533, Western scholars made serious attempts to incorporate the scientific wisdom of the classical world by translating philosophical and scientific works by Jewish, Christian and Muslim scholars from Arabic and Greek into Latin. In this process, they became acquainted with the writings of the great Muslim scientists, such as Al-Khwarizmi, Al-Kindi, Al-Farabi, Ibn Sina, Al-Biruni, Al-Haytham, Al-Razi and Ibn Rushd and gradually acquired an understanding of the "experimental" sciences of the Muslims. In this respect, Alexander Hales and Ramon in the eleventh century, Martin Evak, Raymond, Johannes Hispalensis and John Avendeath of the twelfth century, Roger Bacon, Jacob Anatoli, Michael Scott, Albert the Great and Thomas Aquinas of the thirteenth century, and many others played important roles as translators and promoters of the Muslim scientific tradition. Many words that are now part of the western intellectual tradition were literally translated from Arabic into Latin. Some of these words include nadir, zenith, zero, algebra, and algorithm. Muslim scientists developed their scientific logic from the Qu'ranic mode of evidential argument, which is called *tahdid* ("limits") and *burhan* ("evidence"). In fact, experimental science as a special category of knowledge arose, in part, from methods of reasoning posed by the Qu'ran. During the classical period of Islamic scientific culture in the Middle Ages (primarily the ninth, tenth and eleventh centuries CE), the centers of scientific culture in the Islamic world such as Baghdad and Cordoba incorporated many Jewish and Christian scholars into their learned institutes. They were given the responsibility of translating Greek treatises into Arabic and providing learned commentaries on them. For this reason many scholars now look back at this period as one of *conviviencia* or a peaceful and convivial sharing of a philosophical and scientific culture that was harmonious with the spiritual traditions of Judaism, Christianity and Islam.

Summary and Conclusions

Despite the general belief that the term "science" arose solely from a Greek spirit of learning and Latin linguistic usage, upon scrutiny it was found that *scientia* also evolved from Arabic sources. The Latin words *scientia* and *scientiis* were affected by their translation from the Arabic. Yet, during the latter part of the thirteenth century, Roger Bacon probably invented the phrase *scientia experimentalis* as an equivalent term for the Arabic word *al-ulum at-tajribiyah*, which was rendered into English as "experimental sciences." Even though "experimental sciences" within the context of Bacon's thought is limited to a very rudimentary understanding of the methodology of science, it did start a process of discovery that led to further research into the natural sciences as part of the philosophical discipline of that time. It was not until the sixteenth and the seventeenth centuries that we find a fully-evolved understanding of "science" to mean a rigorous and demonstrable body of knowledge verified by experiments that can be replicated in controlled situations. Even the so-called Scientific Revolution of the seventeenth century still had elements of the traditional view of "science" as part of the realm of natural philosophy and serving as the handmaiden to the realm of theology. Many of the great scientific accomplishments of the sixteenth and seventeenth centuries (such as those represented in cosmology and astronomy by Copernicus and Galileo) were conducted in accordance within the traditional framework of Aristotelian philosophy and the Catholic faith as understood in the Reformation and Counter-Reformation of which they were a part.

It was not until the secularizing trends of the Enlightenment took full control of the intellectual life of Europe that the theological realm was largely severed from the realm of the natural sciences.

---

[1] For the relationship of science and culture, see Science as Culture, http://human-nature.com/science-as-culture/index.html (accessed July 28, 2005).

[2] For a biography of Al Farabi, see http://www.muslimphilosophy.com/farabi/ (accessed July 28, 2005).

[3] For the relationship of science and technology to environmental issues, see *Environmental Science and Technology*. http://www.pubs.acs.org/journalsesthag/.

[4] "Divine providence is God's care, provision, foresight and direction of the universe in such a way that the universe as a whole, and individual creatures within it, fulfil God's purposes. Belief in providence was affirmed by some Greek philosophers (especially the Stoics), and is a fundamental tenet of Judaism, Christianity and Islam." Edward Craig, gen. ed., Routledge Encyclopeida of Philosophy, vol. 7. (London and New York: Routledge, 1998), 797.

[5] "The Enlightenment is frequently portrayed as a campaign on behalf of freedom and reason as against dogmatic faith and its sectarian and barbarian consequences in the history of Western civilization. Many commentators who subscribe to this view find the Enlightenment's cosmopolitan opposition to priestly theology to be dangerously intolerant itself, too committed to uniform ideals of individual self-reliance without regard to community or diversity, or to recasting human nature in the light of science." Ibid., 315.

[6] Lewis T. Charlton, et al, eds. *A Latin Dictionary*, based upon Andrew's edition of Fround's Latin Dictionary, (Oxford, New York, 1879), 1642 – 1643.

[7] Ibid. See also *The World University Encylopedia*, vol. 13, 4514 – 4515.

[8] "Neoplatonism was the final flowering of ancient Greek thought, from the third to the sixth or seventh century AD. Building on eight centuries of unbroken philosophical debate, it addressed questions such as: What is the true self? What is consciousness and how does it relate to reality? Can intuition be reconciled with reason? What are the first causes of reality? How did the universe come into being? How can an efficient cause retain its identity and yet be distributed among its effects? Why does the soul become embodied? What is the good life?" Routledge Encyclopedia of Philosophy, vol. 6. Ibid., 799.

[9] See the *Oxford English Dictionary*, 222.

[10] See William Whewell's *Philosophy of the Inductive Sciences* published in 1840. "During the nineteenth century, 'philosophy of science' or the 'logic of science' became in the writings of William Whewell, John Stuart Mill and others, a main staple of philosophy." Routledge *Encyclopedia of Philosophy*, vol. 8. Ibid., p.578.

[11] John F. Herschel, *Preliminary Discourse on the Study of Natural Philosophy* (Chicago: University of Chicago Press, 1987).

[12] John D. North, Roger Bacon and the Saracenes, 129-16. For a brief discussion of Bacon's place in the history of science and the role of experimental science see David C. Lindberg, The Beginnings of Western Science: The European Scientific Tradition in Philosophical, Religious and Institutional Context, 600 B. C. to A.D. 1450 (Chicago and London: University of Chicago Press, 1992), 226.

[13] F. Copleston, *A History of Philosophy*, vol.2, (Garden City, NY: Doubleday Image, 1962), 71.

[14] Ibid., 78.

[15] Ralph Lerner and Mohsin Mahdi, eds., *Medieval Political Thought: A Source Book* (Canada, 1963), 22.

[16] "Descartes' conception of mind and body represents significant departures from the conceptions of both notions in the late scholastic thought in which he was educated. For the late scholastics working in the Aristotelian tradition, body is composed of matter and form. Matter is that which remains constant in change, while form is that which gives bodies the characteristic properties they have. For Descartes, however, all body is of the same kind of substance that contains only geometric properties, the objects of geometry made concrete.... For the late scholastics, the mind is connected with the account of life. In the Aristotelian view, the soul is the principle of life, that which distinguishes a living thing from a dead thing...For Descartes, the majority of the vital functions are explained in terms of the physical organization of the organic body. The mind, thus, is not a principle of life but a principle of thought." Ibid., vol. 3, 11.

[17] A.C. Crombie, *History of Science* (Mineola, NY: Dover Publications), 38 – 39.

[18] Ibid., 38.

[19] A C Crombie, *Robert Grosseteste and the Origins of Experimental Science* 1100-1700 (Oxford, 1971), 151.

[20] Ibid., 151.

[21] Hossein Nasr, *Science and Civilization in Islam* (Chicago: ABC International Group, 2001), 50.

[22] Ibid., 50.

[23] George Sarton, *Introduction to the History of Science*, vol. 11 (Melbourne, FL: Krieger Publishing Company), 955 – 957.

[24] Op. cit., 49.

[25] Faye Getz, *Medicine in the English Middle Ages* (Princeton, NJ: Princeton University Press, 1998), 39.

[26] Ibid., 67 – 68.

[27] Ibid., p. 61.

[28] Crombie, *Grossteste and theOrigins of Experimental Science*, 139.

[29] Ibid., 191.

[30] Ibid., 192.

[31] Ibid., 191.

[32] Ibid., 192.

[33] A.C. Crombie, *History of Science from Augustine to Galileo* (New York: Dover Publications 1969).

[34] See North, op. cit., 139.

[35] Ibid., 159.

[36] D. Campbell, *Arabian Medicine and its Influence on the Middle Ages*, Trubner's Oriental Series, (Kegan Paul, Trench Trubner and Co. Ltd., 1926), vol. 1, 60.

[37] M. Ullman, *Islamic Survey II, Islamic Medicine* (Edinburgh: Edinburgh University Press, [14], 1978), 46.

[38] Op. cit., 80.

[39] E.J. Dijkesterhuis, *De Mechanisering van het Wereldbeeld* (Amsterdam: Meulenhoff, 1950).

[40] Faye Getz, *Medicine in the Middle Ages* (Princeton, NJ: Princeton University Press, 1998), 53.

Questions for Discussion

1) What do you feel is the proper relationship of Religion and Science in the modern world? Are they complementary or antagonistic to each other? What is the evidence for your point of view?

2) How has the meaning of science evolved from medieval times to our own modern times?

3) What is the significance of Roger Bacon's Latin term *scientia experimentalis*? What is the significant about the difference between the two meanings of the above phrase, *scientia experimentalis*?

4) What is the significance of St. Augustine's theory of knowledge for the medieval understanding of *experiential* knowledge? How did the theory of knowledge affect Roger Bacon's scientific views in his *Opus Majus*? What was the Neoplatonic Doctrine of Illumination that influenced Roger Bacon?

5) Which Islamic authors influenced Roger Bacon and what were their influences?

6) In what way did Descartes' theory of knowledge bear some resemblance to that of St. Augustine? How did the phrase *scientia experimentals* change from the time of Roger Bacon to that of Descartes?

7) What was the scientific method found in Avicenna's *Canon of Medicine*? How did he contribute to the evolution of medicine in the Middle Ages and what impact did he have on the West concerning medical education?

8) Please discuss your understanding of the terms Science and Religion in the light of how we obtain scientific and religious knowledge. Do each of these modes of knowing have distinctive methodologies for discovery of the truth?

Chapter Two

Greek and Hellenistic Roots of Spirituality and Science

The ordered world of the philosophers was known as the *kosmos* from which we get the English word cosmology. The philosophers who introduced these new ways of thinking were called by Aristotle *physikoi* or *physiologoi*, from their concerns with *physis* or nature.

The *Iliad* and *Odyssey* ascribed to Homer describing the tales of the Trojan War between the Greeks and Troy around 1200 BCE were first put to writing around 800 BCE. The *Iliad* recounts the battles of the Trojan War whereas the *Odyssey* describes the wanderings of Odysseus after the Trojan War. The ten-year journey of Odysseus is the myth of the heroic journey that has resonated down through the ages as a primal way of understanding the human encounter with nature. We have the English word "odyssey," which Webster's dictionary defines as a long wandering or voyage usually marked by many changes of fortune or an intellectual or spiritual wandering or quest. The *Odyssey* represents a myth that has continued to influence Western civilization down to our own day. James Joyce's novel, *Ulysses,* and the Charles Frazier novel,

Cold Mountain, continue to capture the imagination of western audiences in both their literary and cinematic forms.[1] "Cold Mountain" is the latest visual reenactment of the Ulysses myth.

The quest for understanding the nature of the physical and spiritual world is part of the leitmotif that has characterized the intellectual history of the Occidental world. Spirituality and science have almost always taken a central place in this quest for meaning (science and wisdom) and transformation (spirituality) that has characterized the soul-work of the West. George Lucas' "Star Wars" is based, in part, on the famous book by Joseph Campbell, *The Hero with a Thousand Faces*[2] and popularized by Bill Moyers in the PBS series on Joseph Campbell. The shamanic vision quest of Native Americans is another example of the heroic journey from that tradition. Space travel is the latest form for the heroic journey with all its perils, as we have seen in the loss of the Columbia space shuttle and its crew during their reentry into the earth's atmosphere on February 1, 2003. The Greek world was populated not just with human beings but with many divinities who interacted with humans through the literary and artistic realms of drama, poetry, song and the visual arts. Zeus was the greatest and most powerful of all the gods and was the lord of the sky and of the weather patterns. Hera was his wife; Poseidon, his brother, was the god of the sea and earth. Hades, another brother of Zeus, was lord of the underworld and of those who had died. Athena was the daughter of Zeus and goddess of warfare. The Greek gods were seen as being directly involved in human affairs and as having a decisive role in determining the outcome of human events. Odysseus had been shipwrecked and imprisoned on an island for eight years before Zeus declared his release so that he could set sail for home in Ithaca. The goddess Gaia (Mother Earth) is now a mythological symbol for many in the environmental movement, symbolizing the life-giving properties of the earth, in stark contrast to the mechanistic and detached approach of a purely physical form of science and technology which dominated much of the nineteenth and twentieth centuries. James Lovelock has attempted to give the Gaia hypothesis a systematic and scientific foundation in his writings.[3] Eros (goddess of love) became the central symbol for the work of Sigmund Freud in his development of analytic psychology and his seminal work, *The Interpretation of Dreams.*[4] These anthropomorphic deities possessed many of the same qualities as human beings, including envy, fear, spite and even hatred. The Greek divinities were capricious in their thoughts and actions and this led to a questioning of the role of the gods within Greek philosophy.

Around the sixth century BCE, a group of men known as philosophers (seekers after wisdom; *sophia* in Greek means wisdom and *philos* means love or lover of wisdom) introduced a new approach to understanding nature and the way that human beings could apprehend the essential meaning of the natural world. They sought to explore the laws of nature not by relying on the intervention of the gods, but by relying solely upon methods of argumentation and proof that were rational in nature. They did not necessarily reject the deities of Greek mythology but considered them to be secondary to the rational mode of inquiry they were following. This inquiry included an investigation into the processes of change and transformation that occurred in the physical world, and the underlying structure of the world and the way that its parts interact. They removed supernatural forces (*deus ex machina*) from their mode of inquiry and focused on predicable and rational principles that might explain the workings of nature. The ordered world of the philosophers was known as the *kosmos* from which we derive the English word "cosmology." "The philosophers who introduced these new ways of thinking were called by Aristotle *physikoi* or *physiologoi*, from their concern with *physis* or nature."[5]

This early group of philosophers was located on the west coast of Asia Minor in the city of Miletus, a Greek colonial area called Ionia (now part of Turkey). Thales, Anaximander and Anaximenes were among this first group of critical thinkers in the recorded history of Western civilization. Thales is reputed to be the first Ionian philosopher who dealt with the fact of changes such as growth, decay and death in nature. He is credited with predicting the solar eclipse that occurred on May 28th, 585 BCE. He may also have introduced the Phoenician practice of steering a ship's course by means of the stars.

According to Aristotle, Thales claimed that the primary component of the universe was water. "In any case the importance of this early thinker lies in the fact that he raised the question, what is the ultimate nature of the world, and not in the answer that he actually gave to the question...."[6] Thales' significance is, in part, his claim that the universe had a fundamental unity amid the plurality of forms we find in nature. Thales conceived of a material substance (water) as the unifying principle, whereas later Greek philosophers would choose other principles that were immaterial in nature, such as the Ideas or Forms of Plato. Heraclitus lived approximately 50 years after Thales; he asserted that fire was the unifying principle. He believed that all reality was in a state of perpetual becoming. All change, for Heraclitus, came about from the interaction of opposing principles. The unifying principles of these opposites were the Logos or immaterial Idea.

According to Fritoj Capra, this initial period of Greek philosophical thought was still holistic in its understanding of spirit and matter.

> The root of physics and of all Western science are to be found in the first period of Greek philosophy in the sixth century B.C., in a culture where science, philosophy and religion were not separated....The Milesians were called "hylozoists," or "those who think matter is alive" by the later Greeks, because they saw no distinction between animate and inanimate, spirit and matter. The monistic and organic view of the Milesians was very close to that of ancient Indian and Chinese philosophy, and the parallels are even stronger in the philosophy of Heraclitus of Ephesus.[7]

Parmenides of Elea was a contemporary of Heraclitus and his critic. He regarded Being as permanent and unchanging. Change was illusory and based on untrustworthy sense experience. Plato would later pick up a similar theme and was united with Parmenides in his critique of sense experience and the illusory character of this type of perception. In order to reconcile the differing philosophies of Heraclitus (Becoming) and Parmenides (Being), the Atomists set forth a theory that tended to separate spirit and matter in order to answer the question of how material reality changes. If the basic building blocks of the universe are atoms, these atoms can be rearranged into different forms but remain essentially the same constitutive parts for the many substances that they constitute. The atoms were inert and passive particles which lacked the vitalism (Vitalists held that living organisms are fundamentally different from non-living entities and usually characterized by a distinctive fluid or "spirit") of earlier Greek philosophy and the more religious or mythological universe expressed in Greek poetry and drama. According to Capra, the separation of spirit and matter, body and soul can be traced back to this period.

> As the idea of a division between spirit and matter took hold, the philosophers turned their attention to the spiritual world, rather than the material, to the human soul and the problem of ethics. These questions were to occupy Western thought for more than two thousand years after the culmination of Greek science and culture in the fifth and fourth centuries B.C.[8]

Another school of thought that included spiritual principles within its philosophical teachings was that of the Pythagoreans, who flourished in the Greek colonies of southern Italy in the sixth and fifth centuries BCE. They claimed that the underlying principle of the universe was numerical in nature. They highlighted the importance of mathematics for understanding the inner meaning of nature. Further, they found this to be particularly evident within the realm of music—for example, the numerical consonance of the musical scale. "Just as musical harmony is dependent on number, so it might be thought that the harmony of the universe depends on number."[9] The Pythagoreans were not only a school of philosophy but a religious community as well, founded by

Pythagoras in the south of Italy during the sixth century BCE. They united an ascetical and spiritual communal life style, a metaphysical understanding of mathematics and a practical application of mathematics to music and geometry. According to Bertrand Russell, the Pythagoreans established the unique combination of theology and human reasoning which would characteristic western culture for centuries to come.

> The combination of mathematics and theology, which began with Pythagoras, characterized religious philosophy in Greece, in the Middle Ages, and in modern times down to Kant....In Plato, St. Augustine, Thomas Aquinas, Descartes, Spinoza and Leibniz there is an intimate blending of religion and reasoning, of moral aspiration with logical admiration of what is timeless, which comes from Pythagoras and distinguishes the intellectualized theology of Europe from the more straightforward mysticism of Asia.[10]

The Atomists, particularly Leucippus and Democritus, felt that the unifying principle consisted of an unlimited number of tiny atoms; this idea seems to prefigure later materialistic explanations of the physical universe. The Atomists represented a shift in thinking from the early Milesians, who retained the essential unity of the material and spiritual realms. "The Greek Atomists drew a clear line between spirit and matter, picturing matter as being made of several 'basic building blocks.' There were purely passive and intrinsically dead particles moving in the void."[11] Western materialism has its roots in the atomistic thought of this group of Milesian philosophers. The question of how spirit related to matter became a central concern in western philosophy over the next 2000 years. The twin giants of the Greek philosophical tradition, Plato and Aristotle and their disciples, became the central interpreters of this question from the fourth century BCE through the sixteenth century CE.

Plato (ca. 427 – 347 BCE), whose real name was Aristocles, was influenced in his early Dialogues by his mentor and esteemed colleague, Socrates, who died in 399 BCE. The death of Socrates is considered a dividing line in the history of philosophy because Socrates formulated new principles of investigation that emphasized political and ethical questions over the cosmological concerns of his day. Socrates developed a critical approach to the traditional values and assumptions of Athenian culture and encouraged his disciples to question established unjust structures or practices and search for values that were consisten with their highest ideals. Plato followed in the footsteps of Socrates and recorded his observations closely; later, Plato established own views in his middle and later Dialogues.

After the death of Socrates at the hands of his political opponents, Plato left Athens for Italy where it is supposed he made contact with Pythagorean communities and their theologians. In 388, Plato returned to Athens and established his own school, the Academy. Plato taught his students through a dialogical method; we have much of his recorded teachings in the form of these dialogues. Plato postulated the existence of a divine craftsman who fabricated the world. This craftsman was called the Demiurge. Just as a carpenter constructs a table or chair according to a mental plan or idea, so also does the divine craftsman (Demiurge) create the universe according to a divine plan or divine Ideas. The Ideas comprise the immaterial "blueprint" for what is found in the sensible world of earthly and material objects. The Ideas, however, are immaterial and incorporeal. They are "essential" reality which allows us to comprehend the true nature of any material substance. The Ideas and the Demiurge are eternal and perfect in their compositions, whereas corporeal objects are impermanent and transitory in nature. The Ideas or Forms are considered primary in their existence in that they do not look to another for their creation or their continuance. Corporeal and sensible objects are considered secondary in their existence because they depend on the Ideas or Forms for identity. In this, sense material or corporal objects were considered to be only a "shadow" of their nature found only in the Ideas or Forms. The true "chair" or "table" is not found in the material embodiment of "chair" or "table" but only in the eternal Form of "chair" or "table."

Plato utilized his allegory of the cave to explain this theory of Ideas or Forms in Book VII of the *Republic*.

> Next, then, I said, "make an image of our nature in its education and want of education, likening it to a condition of the following kind. See human beings as though they were in an underground cave-like dwelling with its entrance, a long one, open to the light across the whole width of the cave. They are in it from childhood with their legs and necks in bonds so that they are fixed, seeing only in front of them, unable because of the bond to turn their heads all the way around. Their light is from a fire burning far above and behind them. Between the fire and the prisoners there is a road above, along which we see a wall, built like the partitions; a puppet-handler, set in front of the human beings and over which they show the puppets....Do you suppose that such men would have seen anything of themselves and one another other than the shadows cast by the fire on the side of the cave facing them?[12]

Plato's theory of nature and his cosmology were largely developed in his dialogue *Timaeus*. Plato was not in agreement with the pre-Socratic philosophers who stressed that nature was governed by its own laws independent of any extrinsic power or divine plan. This clash with the thought of the Atomists would make Plato the favored philosopher for the Patristic Christian world view (the philosophical and theological concepts developed by the Founding Fathers of early Christianity) in which the writings of St. Augustine (ca. 354 – 430) were the most significant. Plato was considered more "spiritual" than any of the Greek philosophers because his understanding of the central role of reason (*Logos*) seemed to be similar in concept to the eternal Word (also *Logos*) of God, said to be incarnate in Jesus Christ. For Plato, reason transcended the purely sensible world of earthly affairs and resided in the eternal realm under the domain of the Demiurge. The Demiurge was the epitome of rationality and the source of beauty, truth and goodness. As the divine craftsman, the Demiurge formed the world from the original chaos of matter, rather than *ex nihilo*, as we find the doctrine of creation expressed in the Book of Genesis. The Demiurge, in some sense, was a supernatural being who acted in a rational and orderly manner but did not have the qualities of personhood that Christianity would ascribe to the triune godhead. The Demiurge relied on mathematical principles in his creative work, for the universe was constructed according to geometrical principles. Plato accepted the teaching of Empedocles that the universe was composed of four elements—earth, water, air and fire—but he claimed that the triangle was the mathematical core of these elements. Here, we can find the Pythagorean influence upon Plato's thought. The variety of elements in the universe allowed for the transformation of substances from one state into another, such as water transforming into air through evaporation. "…Plato's geometrical corpuscles represent a significant step toward the mathematization of nature….Water, air and fire are not *triangular*, they are simply *triangles*. The Pythagorean program of reducing everything to mathematical principles had been fulfilled."[13]

Plato's theory of nature is not a purely rational ordering of material substances. In order to give the world a living quality, the Demiurge creates a "World-Soul" for the earth and "souls" for each of the planets. The "soul" is the principle of intelligibility and "mindfulness" that gives life to inanimate objects on earth or in the heavens. Plato also postulates that human beings have souls, as well; they are similar in nature to those which inform the earth and the heavens. The soul is the center for the action of the mind (*nous*) which governs all human appetites and provides a rational foundation for society.

Plato does not affirm or deny the existence of the Greek deities that inhabited Mount Olympus. It is clear that Plato's rationalism was not the governing compass for most of the Greek population who probably still believed in the intervention of the gods, whether for good or ill, into their daily lives. For example, Greek medical practice focuses on rational procedures to restore a patient's health but these "scientific" medical practices do not rule out the continued presence and popularity of healing deities and healing centers throughout Greece and its colonies. Plato had his vociferous critics, however, for he seemed to find slavery an acceptable practice and many find his "spiritualization" of the material world an unscientific hypothesis without justification.

> Plato, who believed that "all things are full of gods," actually used the metaphor of slavery to connect his politics with his cosmology....In the recognition by Pythagoras and Plato that the Cosmos is knowable, that there is a mathematical underpinning to nature, they greatly advanced the cause of science. But in the suppression of disquieting facts, the sense that science should be kept for a small elite, the distaste for experiment and the easy acceptance of slave societies, they set back the human enterprise.[14]

Plato's epistemology does not reject the value of sense experience, for he felt such expression could lead to knowledge of the Ideas or Forms through his doctrine of reminiscence. In this way, the soul could recollect experiences of the Forms even if these took place in the past, perhaps even in a past life. Plato justifies the study of astronomy and geometry because he felt these investigations led the soul more easily to the realm of the Forms. Plato seems to have accepted the Pythagorean belief that sense knowledge is relative and imperfect because it is always in a state of becoming. He agreed with Socrates that the true object of knowledge must be judgments about *universals.* In the later Middle Ages, the Nominalists claimed that only *individuals* were real. If someone claimed that Socrates was a "good" person, the concept of goodness must be stable and permanent for all who share in this goodness. The same would be true for someone who was considered to be a "bad" person. Scientific knowledge, for Plato, needed to be expressed in clear and distinct definitions of universal concepts. Knowledge of particular objects (such as this person or this chair) would be of a much lower order than knowledge of the essential "humanity" of this person or the essential "chairness" of this chair. These universals have objective reality in the world of Ideas or Forms.

Aristotle took exception to the doctrine of Ideas and formulated his own epistemological theory to answer the question of how the mind is able to know universal concepts. According to Plato, the human mind has two forms of apprehension of external objects: _doxa_ (opinion) and _episteme_ (knowledge). _Doxa_ only deals with "images" or "copies" of external objects whereas _epistme_ directly apprehends the universal concept or its Form. For example, we may see examples of goodness in a particular person who does good works, but most of these examples are only "images" of true goodness. If we apprehend "goodness in itself" or its essential nature, we attain to the Form or Idea of goodness itself.

According to Aristotle, Plato held that mathematical concepts were "between" forms and sensible things. Further, besides sensible things and forms, he says there are the objects of mathematics, which occupy an intermediate position, differing from sensible things (being eternal and unchangeable), from Forms in that there are many alike, while the Form itself is in each case unique.[15] Plato seemed to hold that a mathematical concept, such as the circle, is neither a sensible particular nor pure Form but something in a middle zone between the sensible world of individual objects (such as a circular building) and the pure Form of "circleness." The concept of "circle" in mathematics, particularly geometry, partakes of an intelligibility that seemed of a higher order to Plato and those who followed his basic teachings. For this reason, the realm of mathematics was seen as a more "spiritual" realm of thought because it seemed closer to the sphere of the Forms. In this sense, Plato may have been partly influenced by the Pythagorean reverence for numbers since he had contact with them on his visit to the south of Italy. We shall see the same connection between mathematics and Neoplatonic thought in the writings of the Augustinian philosophers of the thirteenth century CE, Robert Grosseteste and Roger Bacon. They were among the first to explore the meaning of *scientia experimentalis* (experimental science) in the western world, although many of their philosophical concepts were indebted to the mediating influence of Islamic philosophers whose writings were translated from Arabic into Latin in the twelfth and thirteenth centuries. Grosseteste and Bacon were not empiricists in the sense that Francis Bacon would use the term in his famous work, *Novum Organon*, nor were they "experimental" in the sense that Galileo understood his own experimental methods. They did, however, break new ground in the field of optics, which they understood in the "light" of the Augustinian doctrine of divine illumination. According to Nasr, "A few northern European scientists and philosophers like Roger Bacon were to combine observation of nature with a mystical philosophy based on illumination...."[16] The Augustinian tradition of illumination became part of the epistemological context for the exploration of *scientia experimentalis* at Oxford University during the thirteenth and fourteenth centuries.

> Augustinian thought, with its strong Platonic emphasis on mathematics as the clearest example of the divine truth or wisdom, was found very congenial to the Arabic version of Neoplatonism, which had directed their mathematical interests much more to the interpretation of nature. Under the double influence of mathematics and the Arabian developments of practical science, there existed from 1200 on a strong current of scientific Augustinism, side by side with the theological and mystical Augustinism of the twelfth-century schools, and often combined in the same man, as with Roger Bacon.[17]

Bacon's work symbolized this early blending of spirituality with science at the beginning of the scholastic philosophical tradition in the thirteenth century. This tradition would dominate the next three centuries of European intellectual history. The impact would even be felt in the work of Martin Luther in the sixteenth century. One of Luther's influences was William of Ockham, who also stood within this Augustinian and Neoplatonic tradition. The University of Oxford would play a central role in the development of this school of thought, which greatly influenced the emergence of modern science in the sixteenth and seventeenth centuries.

Bacon and his successors did not clearly separate the worlds of spirituality and science and, in fact, saw them as interdependent. The separation of spirit and matter would largely occur in the thought of Descartes in the seventeenth century and become part of a purely physical and mechanical interpretation of nature by many of the Enlightenment thinkers of the eighteenth century. Some scholars see the thirteenth century as the "golden age" of Scholasticism (a philosophical movement that dominated Western Christendom in the Middle Ages which was heavily influenced by Aristotelian categories of thought), for it witnessed the creation of an intellectual synthesis of faith and science in the work of philosopher/theologians such as Albert the Great and Thomas Aquinas. In the following century, a kind of intellectual doubt began to enter into Western philosophy with the nominalistic[18] teachings of William of Ockham.

> Ockham created a theologism which destroyed the certainty of medieval philosophy and led to a philosophical skepticism. Meanwhile, in emphasizing particular universal causes and criticizing Peripatetic philosophy and science, Ockham and his followers like Oresme and Nicolas of Autrecourt made important discoveries in mechanics and dynamics, discoveries that form the basis of the seventeenth-century revolution in physics."[19]

Aristotle (384 – 322 BCE) was the unsurpassed polymath of the ancient world. His influence extended through the Middle Ages to the birth of the modern world in the sixteenth century. He was born in Stagira, but was sent to Athens to study under Plato. He remained a member of Plato's Academy for approximately 20 years until Plato's death in ca. 347 BCE. He then spent several years traveling, a time when he concentrated on his biological research. He returned from what is now the nation of Turkey to Macedonia where he became the tutor of Alexander the Great. He returned to Athens about 335 and established his own philosophical school which met in a public garden called the Lyceum. Aristotle's "philosophical academy" was also called the Lyceum. He was in exile toward the end of life but continued teaching until his death in 322.

Aristotle's prolific writings were encyclopedic in nature and about thirty of his writings are still extant. Some of the works attributed to him are contested. Even though he had great respect for Plato and admired his integrity and high idealism, he did not agree with the Platonic doctrine of Ideas or Forms and Plato's diminishment of the sensible and material world. George Sarton's critique of the Platonic suprasensible world of forms was shared by Aristotle. For Aristotle, the essence of a table or chair lay within the table or chair and not in the eternal world of Forms. The attributes of a table or chair (such as construction out of a particular type of wood), belonged to the particular chairs or table under consideration. Individual sensible objects are called "substances" by Aristotle. The "substance" is, for Aristotle, the subject to which its properties must adhere. For example, a piece of bread has color, texture and taste but these are properties of the substance called "bread," also called "accidents" by Aristotle to distinguish them from the essential quality of bread. This distinction would become very important in the Middle Ages because of the Catholic Church's doctrine of Transubstantiation of the bread and wine at Mass into the Body and Blood of Christ. This doctrinal formulation relied heavily on the Aristotelian distinction between "substance" and "accidents."

In the Church's teaching, the substance of Christ's Body remained after the words of consecration, but the accidents of bread and wine (color, shape and texture) were unchanged. The doctrine of Transubstantiation became central to the Catholic understanding of how faith and science could complement one another. St. Thomas, the Angelic Doctor of the Church, relied upon Aristotelian categories to explain this mystery of faith.

Aristotle's epistemology was based on the trustworthy nature of sensible experience. Plato distrusted the sensible world of change and flux whereas Aristotle believed that by repeated observation of any individual substance a person could, through an inductive process, discover or elicit its underlying universal or common structure that gave it an identity, which then corresponded to similar traits in other similar, individual substances. Once this likeness was discovered, it was possible to affirm a universal proposition which could form the foundation for *deductive* reasoning. Deductions can move from either universal to particular claims or from particular to universal claims.

Aristotle put this form of reasoning into a logical structure called a syllogism, comprised of major and minor premises, a middle term and a conclusion. For example, the universal statement, "all men are mortal" is the major premise; "Aristotle is a man" is the minor premise and the conclusion is "Aristotle is a mortal thing." The major term appears on the right of the conclusion ("mortal thing") and the minor term is on the left of the conclusion ("Aristotle"). The middle term in this syllogism is "man" and it is the common term in the major and minor premises.

Another way of understanding Aristotle's form of deductive reasoning would be to state "If a quality (A) belongs to the subject (B) and the subject (B) belongs to the subject (C) then (A) belongs to the subject (C) as well as (B)." The subject term is on the left and the predicate term is on the right. In order to show that a syllogism is valid it is necessary to show the relationship between the two terms of the syllogism (subject of the major premise and the attribute or predicate of the conclusion). This syllogistic form of reasoning presumed that deductive universal premises could be then applied to particular instances. Aristotle presumed that the conclusion of a valid syllogism expressed the necessary relation between two terms in the form of a definition. Even though modern philosophers question the necessity of the connection between major and minor premises as understood by Aristotle, this form of scientific reasoning remained dominant in Western thought until the Scientific Revolution of the sixteenth and seventeenth century. It also became commonplace in the medieval universities and even influenced the work of Galileo in the sixteenth century.[20]

Aristotle's theory of change was based on his theory of nature. He believed that an inner seminal force was located within each substance that enabled each "form" in nature to grow, much like an acorn grows into a mature tree. Each substance was constituted of "matter" and "form." The "form" expressed the essential nature of the object whereas matter was a passive recipient of the "form" or its essential nature. The "form" of man was located within the nature of each particular man or woman. Unlike Plato, Aristotle believed that "form" was not an extrinsic and eternal immaterial reality, but was located on the earthly plane and found in each individual who shared this essential nature.

Aristotle also held that the "form" could move from potentiality to actuality just as an acorn grows into a tree. Change, therefore, was not accounted for by external forces but rather by the internal dynamism of nature itself. Aristotle did not feel a need for the experimental method that would later become the standard for modern science. His reasoning process did not require such a method because he felt that all natural objects reflected their inner natures by their behavior. Therefore, a detailed study of the activities which characterized the functioning of objects in nature could reveal their essential character and purpose.

Purposefulness, or *teleology*, was another important aspect of Aristotle's thought. He felt that all of nature was bound together by an inherent design or purpose that would be expressed in the activity of the object or objects under consideration. It should be noted that Descartes rejected this idea of final cause in his more mechanical understanding of the material universe in the seventeenth century.

From the fourth century BCE until the seventeenth century CE, Aristotle's understanding of natural causality dominated philosophical and scientific thought in the western world. Aristotle claimed four levels of causality to explain the process of change in the world. In any change of state, such as water evaporating into air, the matter does not change but its form does change from the form of water to the form of air. There is also an agent or agency that brings about this change (such as the warming of water by the sun), which is called the material cause of the transformation of water into air. The new form brought about by the change of state is called the formal cause and the agency effecting the change (the sun warming the water) is called the efficient cause. Finally, and most importantly, the purpose served by the change is called the final cause. Final causality is a key metaphysical concept that would inform much of the medieval understanding of the divine purpose in creating the world and human beings. When this type of causality was removed from scientific thinking in the seventeenth century, it led to questioning the involvement of the godhead in creating and sustaining the material universe. Aristotle held that final causality had priority over material causality because the purpose for a chair or table precedes its construction from a piece of wood. Without a clear purpose for the wood in his mind, the carpenter could not construct the chair or table. In this sense, the final cause for the table or chair stood ahead of the actual construction of these functional objects. Aristotle's view of nature also stood in contrast to that of the Atomists, who viewed the world more mechanically and without any clear internal design. Aristotle's cosmology also included a sophisticated understanding of how each of the different spheres of the cosmos (the earthly, lunar and celestial) had its own unique purpose. Aristotle understood the universe to be eternal in nature and comprised of a great sphere divided into upper and lower regions. The lunar sphere acted as an intermediary zone between the terrestrial and celestial spheres. The earthly sphere was dominated by the transitions from birth to death of organic beings, plus other types of changes such as fluctuating weather patterns, earthquakes, floods and the rise and fall of civilizations. The celestial sphere, however, did not change and was dominated by the unchanging eternal cycles of the starry heavens. In his *De Coelo* (*On Heaven*), Aristotle states that "in the whole range of time past, so far as our inherited records reach, no change appears to have taken place in the whole scheme of the outermost heaven or in any of its proper parts."[21] According to Aristotle, the heavens were filled with a fifth element called "aether." Aristotle claimed that a void was impossible in the heavens and that the whole heavenly sphere was filled with aether. The earth, of course, stood at the center of the universe with the lunar and celestial spherical shells surrounding it. Aristotle accepted the four elements of Plato and Empedocles (earth, water, air and fire) as the essential building blocks of the earthly realm. He did not agree, however, with Plato's Pythagorean theory of the triangle as the ultimate character of material substances. Aristotle claimed that four qualities, (hot and cold; wet and dry), were the primordial building blocks of material reality. In addition to these four primordial elements, Aristotle added the attribute of "light" or "heavy." Earth and water were heavy and, therefore, moved toward the center of the universe. Air and fire are light; they tended to move toward the outer spheres of the universe.

According to Aristotle, the variety of substances that filled the cosmos left no void. In this matter of the void or its opposite, the *plenum* (meaning the fullness of the universe), Aristotle was opposed to the views of the Atomists who viewed the atoms as moving through spatial voids during a process of change. Aristotle asserted that there is no motion without a mover. He held that there were two types of motion: natural and forced. Natural motion flows from the nature of the body and when it reaches its destination, motion ceases. In his *Physics,* Aristotle claimed that when two bodies of differing weights descended, the time required to cover the distance would be inversely proportional to their weight. He also held that resistance could slow the rate of motion in proportion to the level of resistance.

The concept of velocity was not present in Aristotle's thought but would become part of the medieval contribution to the question of motion and how substances change under various conditions. Modern mechanics does not acknowledge any differences in nature and treats all objects as essentially identical for purposes of its investigations According to Aristotle, the celestial region has seven stars: the sun, moon, Mercury, Venus, Mars, Jupiter, and Saturn. The stars received their initial movements from the "Unmoved Mover" or the "Prime Mover." In order to explain this within his philosophy of nature and causality, Aristotle postulated that each of the celestial spheres had its own "Prime Mover," based on final causality rather than efficient causality, since the spheres were eternal in nature. In his *History of Animals,*[22] Aristotle "laid the foundations of systematic zoology and (his research and analysis) have profoundly shaped thought on human biology for some two thousand years."[23] Aristotle's work was mainly a catalogue of more than 500 species of animals and descriptive in nature. His observational skills were unmatched for his time and his documentation of the behaviors of many species was unrivalled for centuries. He relied heavily on his theory of final causality to explain the processes of growth and maturation in animals. For this reason, he felt that research in the animal kingdom must note the mature state of the organism, since the growth of the organism into its mature state is the key to understanding even its earlier states of being. The limits of Aristotle's scientific method are found in his deductive and syllogistic methods of reaching formal and necessary conclusions. He felt that science can only demonstrate conclusively those qualities that necessarily belong to a subject's essence. In this form of reasoning, the cause of the conclusion is found within the demonstration itself. Aristotle was not completely consistent with his deductive methods because he did use other more inductive forms of reasoning in his writings on the natural sciences, such as those on biology. He did generally hold, however, that real scientific knowledge had to be about universals and not about individuals. Qualities common to many individuals could become a universal statement but this "form" was not a separately existing "Form" as found in Plato but rather something (an attribute of a substance) found "in common" with all the individuals in this class.[24]

Aristotle's intellectual prowess covered so many areas and contained so many seminal insights and observations that he remained the single greatest philosopher affecting the intellectual history of the western world through the Renaissance. His contributions covered metaphysics, natural philosophy, epistemology, cosmology, biology, geology, optics and planetary astronomy. His philosophy of nature included a metaphysical explanation of its purpose which would be one of his most significant contributions to natural theology. We shall examine in some detail how the teleological framework he provided to metaphysics formed the essential core of much of the Scholastic Era's understanding of the divine purpose at work in the world. In this sense, Aristotle helped to frame many of the later arguments for the providential character of the divine purpose in designing the universe and the human race. The Scholastics had serious problems with the fact that Aristotle held to the belief that the world and the universe were eternal in nature. This aspect of his teaching collided with the biblical accounts of creation found in Genesis. The teachings of the Hebrew and Christian scriptures presume a *creatio ex nihilo* whereas the Aristotelian universe lacked such a theory of origins for the material world. The Book of Genesis states that the physical words owes its existence to a transcendent deity, but for Aristotle the material world always existed and had no initial starting point.

As another point of transition between the Hellenistic world that preceded the first centuries of the Christian era, we will examine how the healing traditions of Greek and Christian communities may have differed and how they may be understood in the light of contemporary psychology and spirituality. The healing tradition of Christianity provides us with a point of comparison with that of the earlier Greek culture and its Hellenistic and Roman manifestations in which healing and medicine played important roles.

The Greek healing traditions of antiquity revolved around the Greek god of medicine known as Asclepius (called Aesculapius in the Roman world). He was considered the son of Apollo and was worshipped throughout Greece, although his central shrine was located in Epidaurus, in northeastern Peloponnese. The mythology of Asclepius' healing ability seemed to flow from his amazing birth. He was born in the wilderness where he was guarded by a supernatural light that shone over him. At his appointed time he began a mission of teaching his healing arts and imparting his medical knowledge. According to the myth, Asclepius' teacher was the Centaur Chiron. Asclepius had such amazing power that he could bring his patients back to life. Hades, the god of the underworld, was so upset by the power of Asclepius to restore life that he feared Asclepius would lessen his power over the Underworld and remove the souls under his control. Zeus agreed with Hades' complaint and struck Asclepius dead with a thunderbolt. After his death, Asclepius "ascended" into the heavens and became the god of healing powers. We can see many parallels in this story to the healing traditions of Christianity as found in the miraculous healing powers of Jesus expressed in the New Testament. The center of the Asclepian cult was Epidaurus, but other important sanctuaries were located in Pergamum and Cos. Cos was also the home of Hippocrates, considered the founder of Western medicine and the Hippocratic Oath. The sanctuary of Asclepius became an international healing center much like Fatima and Lourdes are today. We have examples of cures ascribed to Asclepius in a series of tablets found at the sanctuary of Asclepius in Epidaurus. Six of these tablets were described by Pausania in the second century CE, and depicted miraculous cures performed by Asclepius. In one cure a voiceless boy is restored after performing the correct sacrifice to Asclepius; in another cure, a growth on a boy's neck is healed when one of the temple dogs licks it. Some of the Epidaurus suppliants see a "vision-in-sleep" (*enhypnion*), the same word used by Galen in *On Diagnosis in Dreams* (see Chapter Four for more on Galen).

This sanctuary continued as the center of the festival called *Ascleia* from the fifth century BCE until well into the Roman era. Patients who came to the festival would spend the night in dormitories which were dedicated to Asclepius, and where patients would experience dream-like periods of contact with the god. This encounter with Asclepius in the night was called "incubation." Asclepius would appear in the patient's dream and given him or her advice about their illness. In the morning, the Asclepian priests would interpret the dream and provide a regimen of healing for the patient.

Statues of Asclepius showed him holding a staff with a serpent intertwined around the staff. (see the following web link: **http://www.maicar.com/GML/ Asclepius.html**, for an image of Asclepius:). The caduceus, the image of twin snakes wrapped around a staff with two wings at the top, has been the symbol of healing for the medical profession since the time of the Greeks. The caduceus or *Kerykeon* was known in Greek mythology as the magic rod of Hermes, the Greek messenger of the Gods. According to legend, Hermes came across two battling snakes and threw his magic wand at them. They became entwined and stopped fighting. This legend may have led to the symbol of two intertwined snakes and the wings of Hermes the messenger above the snakes. Some Gnostic Christians worshipped the serpent hung on a cross as the "Tree of Life." We find mention of the serpent as a healing symbol in the story of Moses and the bronze serpent.

> At this God sent fiery serpents among the people; their bite brought death to many in Israel. The people came and said to Moses, "We have sinned by speaking against Yahweh and against you. Intercede for us with Yahweh to save us from these serpents." Moses interceded for the people, and Yahweh answered him, "Make a fiery serpent and put it on a standard. If anyone is bitten and looks at it, he shall live." So Moses fashioned a bronze

serpent which he put on a standard, and if anyone was bitten by a serpent, he looked at the bronze serpent and lived. (Numbers: 21:6-9, *New Jerusalem Bible*).

It is interesting to note the contrast between the serpent found in the Hebrew and Christian mythology of the Garden of Eden (in which the snake symbolizes the temptation of disobey God) and the Greek mythology of the serpent in which he symbolizes renewal and regeneration. According to some scholars, the original Neolithic myth of the goddess had a Mother/Creator Goddess and the Serpent as her consort. The Serpent was not a seducer but rather a source of life and wholeness.[25] In the Sumerian cities of Ur and Uruk (now part of Iraq), two images of the Goddess and her children were found; both children had the heads of snakes. The snake was also a phallic symbol that could impregnate the Goddess *and* be her son and consort in endless cycles of regeneration.[26]

The serpent has long been a symbol for healing, regenerative forces. Spiritual disciplines such as yoga, tantra, tai chi and other practices are examples of those practices that can awaken the "inner serpent." The snake's ability to seemingly regenerate itself by sloughing off its skin every few months has continued for centuries as a symbol of healing and regeneration. In addition, it has the ability to carry venom (a symbol of power) yet not poison itself. The snake seems to be an archetypal image that appears in all cultures and from all periods of history. The image of the snake also shows how the healing powers of nature are integrated into these earlier cultures through various types of mythological events.

These myths represent a profound truth about how we actually are healed. Recent studies in holistic medicine indicate that the healing process is complex and involves the subjectivity of the patient. Imagery is an important aspect of healing, often appearing in a patient's dreams. The Greek healing centers utilized the dream process much as Jungian analysts do in Western psychology. Transpersonal psychology and holistic medicine are beginning to explore the wisdom of the ages that we now find has a scientific and phenomenological foundation. The unconscious life of the patient divulged in his or her dream life reflects the powerful energy-laden images that may control subjective states of mind and may also control much of the immune system. Studies in cancer patients who survive over long periods of time indicate that the interior states of consciousness may have as much to do with healing as any external treatment by Western medicine.[27] The healing powers of nature, such as we find in the serpent symbol, are expressed in Shamanic healing and in the mythology that surrounds it. Nature herself has the power to heal her children. Within the Inca tradition of the South American Andes, the Shamans draw their healing powers from the elements of nature found in various herbs and the cocoa leaf. The personification of nature is highlighted with her names, Pacha Mama or Mother Earth.[28]

Medical science is beginning to see the relationship between spirituality and healing. Many studies have indicated that a person with a strong belief system tends to have a higher recovery rate from life-threatening illnesses than those who lack such resources. Other studies indicate a relationship between prayer and healing even when those prayed for were at a distance from those who intended recovery through intercessory prayer.

One explanation for these occurrences is

> ...that the mind is non-local and that under special conditions its non-local nature is manifested. According to this view, energy or information does not "travel" from one place to another or from one mind to another, but is already "everywhere." The influencer's mind and the subject's mind may not really be as distinct, separate and isolated as they appear to be but, rather, may be profoundly interconnected, unified, omnipresent and omniscient.... The existence of such connections is compatible with the ontological, epistemological, and ethical teachings of many of the world's religious, spiritual, meditative and mystical traditions.[29]

It is not necessary to agree with the specific ontological suppositions of "omnipresence and omniscience" in order to accept the validity of intercessory prayer, but we do know that human communication is multidimensional and mysterious. We cannot limit communication and communion among humans and nature to a purely physical model without contradicting most of the insights of the great religious traditions of the world.

The shamanic tradition of communion with the spirit world of nature has been largely eliminated from our technological society, yet it is reappearing in the therapeutic and healing arts of alternative medicine and is increasing in popularity in the Western world. The worlds of the imagination the unconscious have been the vehicles for accessing this transpersonal and archetypal form of consciousness. "Our contemporary fascination with shamanism is an expression of a hunger for experiences that engage and satisfy the total spectrum of life, and not just the human dimension. The shamanic perspective affirms the archetypal nature of the primal expressions in the pictures, dances, sounds, and dramas emerging from our art therapy studios."[30] The Greek island of Cos was home to one of the greatest figures in the history of the Western medical arts, Hippocrates (460 – 370 BCE). We have many writings ascribed to Hippocrates. None of them, however, can be traced directly to him but rather to those who were considered his disciples. For this reason we speak of the "Hippocratic Corpus" numbering between sixty and seventy volumes. These writings were characterized by a more naturalistic and philosophical frame of reference than the supernatural qualities of the healing craft that we see in the Asclepian cult. By the time of Hippocrates, medicine was beginning to establish standards of conduct and methods of practice that would lead, many centuries later, to the medical profession with its own ethical codes and approved methods of training and supervision. At the time of Hippocrates, few professional standards were in place and many charlatans were making false claims about their healing powers. The noted Hippocratic Oath, the canonical oath for the medical profession first composed around 400 BCE, is still in use today, although in a variety of modified forms. The Oath opens with the statement that the aspiring physician "swears" his oath "by Apollo, the physician, and Aesculapius, (or Asclepius) and Health, and All-heal, and the gods and goddesses."[31]

The Oath presumes that medicine is still an "art" and that the physician is required to live a virtuous life: "With purity and holiness I will pass my life and practice my art."[32] The physician's Oath includes the vow to pass on this knowledge to others "without fee or stipulation" and to "abstain from every voluntary act of mischief and corruption." The physician, similar to a priest in later ages, must keep inviolate any information about his patients that "should be kept secret." It is clear from the tenor of the Oath that the physician is expected to have a strong sense of spirituality and service to others as part of the vocation for this profession. Because of the unregulated nature of medical practice in the ancient world, the Hippocratic Oath and the writings which followed were meant to elevate the profession and discourage those who were unscrupulous and unqualified from practicing this art.

In one of the Hippocratic writings, *On the Sacred Disease,* the author rebukes those who call an illness "sacred" simply to hide their own lack of knowledge about disease. "These are exactly the people who pretend to be very pious and to be particularly wise. By invoking a divine element they were able to screen their own failure to give suitable treatment and so called this a 'sacred' malady to conceal their own ignorance of its nature."[33] The philosophy of the Hippocratic writings presumes that there is a natural cause for any illness and that it is not due to some divine intervention in the person's life. The cause of illness was usually associated with some type of imbalance in the bodily fluids, presumed to be composed of blood, phlegm, yellow bile and black bile. Each of these four humors was connected with the qualities of hot and cold, and moist and dry. The physician's role was to prescribe the correct regimen to help bring the body back into balance. The most common "regimen" included suggestions about changes in diet, types of exercise, sleeping patterns, bathing rituals and exposure to certain environments that might be beneficial (such as the ocean or the forest.) Today, we would consider this type of medical consultation as preventive in nature. Hippocratic physicians did, however, engage in clinical case histories which helped them develop a systematic approach to certain types of illnesses and medical conditions. Many of the remedies prescribed by physicians in this period of history were herbal in nature. Physicians could also prescribe stronger remedies if they felt that the patient's bodily fluids were severely imbalanced. In such cases, they would use purification procedures to help restore balance in the bodily fluids. These procedures could include emetics (agents that induce vomiting), blood-letting, purgatives and enemas, or diuretics.

Usually the "scientific" physician provided his service to those who were able to pay his fees, since there was no government or community-supported health care system. The lower classes usually relied on the healing temples for treatment, which included a limited amount of herbal remedies to complement the divination methods that were part of the incubation period in the Asclepian Temples.[34] This early Greek concept of "balance" in the human body resembles contemporary theories of "balance" relating to management of stress in a person's life. The famed University of Massachusetts Medical Center Stress Reduction and Relaxation Program, or "stress clinic," has been a pioneer in the field of behavioral medicine. The underlying assumption of the stress clinic is that imbalance in bodily systems, (not necessarily, as the Greeks believed, bodily fluids), correlate very strongly with certain types of chronic diseases such as high blood pressure, back pain, heart disease, cancer and AIDS. The treatment at this clinic is "based on rigorous and systematic training in mindfulness, a form of meditation originally developed in the Buddhist tradition in Asia."[35]

The underlying philosophy of this clinic has much in common with the early Greek notion of "balance," although "balance" in contemporary usage is viewed in a wider context than the Greeks thought possible. David Bohm, the noted theoretical physicist, has focused much of his work on wholeness as a fundamental datum of nature. The words "medicine" and "meditation" come from the Latin *mederi*, which means "to cure." *Mederi* itself derives from an earlier Indo-European word meaning "to measure."[36] Bohm claims that all things have "their own inward measure." Meditation, then, in the sense of "right measure" is the method we can use to restore our being to a non-judgmental and supportive state that we call wholeness of mind, body and spirit. Albert Einstein alluded to this larger wholeness in his famous letter he wrote to a nineteen-year-old girl who had recently lost her sister.

> A human being is a part of the whole, called by us "Universe," a part limited in time and space. He experiences himself, his thoughts and feelings as something separated from the rest—a kind of optical delusion of his consciousness. This delusion is a kind of prison for us, restricting us to our personal desires and to affections for a few persons nearest to us. Our task must be to free ourselves from this prison by widening our circle of compassion to embrace all living creatures and the whole nature in its beauty. Nobody is able to achieve this completely, but the striving for such achievement is in itself a part of the liberation, and a foundation for inner security.[37]

[1] "Cold Mountain", the film directed by Anthony Minghella, was released on December 25, 2003 by Miramax Films to much acclaim. See also Jack Kerouac's On the Road for another literary of the heroic journey.

[2] Joseph Campbell, *The Hero with a Thousand Faces* (Princeton: Princeton University Press, 1990).

[3] James Lovelock, *Gaia: A New Look at Life on Earth* (Oxford: Oxford University Press, 1995). See also *The Age of Gaia: A Biography of the Living Earth* (Oxford: Oxford University Press, 1996).

[4] Sigmund Freud, *The Interpretation of Dreams: Authorized Translation of Third Edition with Introduction by A.A. Brill* (New York: Barnes and Noble, 1994).

[5] David Lindberg, *The Beginnings of Western Science* (Chicago: University of Chicago Press, 1992), 27.

[6] Frederick Copleston, *A History of Philosophy, vol. I, "Greece and Rome," part I* (New York: Doubleday Image, 1960), 39.

[7] Fritjof Capra, *The Tao of Physics* (Berkeley: Shambala, 1975), 20.

[8] Ibid., 21.

[9] Copleston, Ibid., 49.

[10] Ibid., 21. Text found in *History of Western Philosophy* by Bertrand Russell.

[11] Lindberg, Ibid., 21.

[12] Alan Bloom, trans., *The Republic of Plato, with Notes and Interpretive Essay* (New York: Basic Books, 1968), 193.

[13] Ibid., 41.

[14] Carl Sagan, *Cosmos* (New York: Ballantine Books, 1985), 186. PBS presented an award-winning series based upon the themes found in this book.

[15] See Aristotle's *Metaphysics*.

[16] Seyyed Hossein Nasr, *Man and Nature: The Spiritual Crisis in Modern Man* (Chicago: ABC International Group, 1997), 60.

[17] John H. Randall, Jr., *Career of Philosophy, vol. 1* (NY: Columbia University, 1962), 259. Augustinian thought emphasized divine predestination and the necessity of divine grace for any truly moral action. His theories of divine illumination flowed from his emphasis on divine grace over any human effort.

[18] "Nominalism refers to a reductionist approach to problems about the existence and nature of abstract entities; it thus stands opposed to Platonism and realism....Nominalists like Abelard and Ockham insisted that everything that exists is particular. They argued that talk of universals is talk about certain linguistic expressions." *Routledge Encylopedia of Philosophy.* vol. 7 (London and New York: Routledge, 1998), 17 – 18.

[19] Seyyed Hossein Nasr, *Man and Nature: The Spiritual Crisis in Modern Man* (Chicago: ABC International Group, 1997), 63.

[20] For a detailed discussion of how Aristotelian logic influenced Galileo see William A. Wallace's *Galileo's Logic of Discovery and Proof,* (Dordrecht, Netherlands: Springer Dordrecht, 1992).

[21] Lindberg, 55.

[22] Aristotle's *History of Animals* can be viewed at http://classics.mit.edu/Aristotle/history_anim.6.vi.html (accessed 7/28/05).

[23] Op. cit., 62.

[24] For a discussion of Aristotle's scientific method of demonstration see "Aristotle" by Richard Bodeus in *The Columbia History of Western Philosophy*, Richard H. Popkin, ed. (New York: MJF Books, 1999), 62 – 64.

[25] Anne Baring and Jules Cashford, *The Myth of the Goddess* (London: Viking, 1991).

[26] See the "Goddess and the Snake" by Katherine Woodworth, www.acqufemina.com.

[27] Lawrence LeShan, Ph.D. *Cancer as a Turning Point* (New York: Penguin, 1990), and Bernie Segal, *Love, Medicine and Miracles* (New York: Harper and Row, 1988).

[28] See www.windows.ucar.edu/tour/link=/mythology/pachamama_earth.html.

[29] William Brand, Ph. D., "Empirical Explorations of Prayer, Distant Healing and Remote Mental Influence," *Journal of Religion and Psychical Research* 17, no. 2 (April 1994).

[30] Shaun McNiff, *Art as Medicine: Creating a Therapy of the Imagination.* (Boston: Shambhala Publications, 1992).

[31] Hippocratic Oath translated by Francis Adams: www.classics.mit.edu/Hippocrates'hippooath.html.

[32] Ibid.

[33] Lindberg, op. cit., 116.

[34] I am grateful for the insights of the Stanford University Online History of Medicine coursed developed by Stanford Humanities Scholar Elissa Meites.

[35] Jon Kabat-Zinn, *Full Catastrophe Living: Using the Wisdom of Your Body and Mind to Face Stress and Illness* (New York: Dell, 1990), 2.

[36] Ibid., 163.

[37] Ibid., 165.

Questions for Discussion

1) What were some of the characteristic views about nature among the pre-Socratic philosophers in ancient Greece?

2) What view of nature do we find in the philosophy of Plato?

3) What view of nature do we find in the philosophy of Aristotle?

4) In what way did a rational understanding of nature complement or conflict with a more supernatural understanding as reflected in the healing cult of Asclepius?

5) What were some important characteristics of the healing traditions in ancient Greece?

6) What role did dreams play in these healing traditions?

7) What kinds of symbols were prominent in the ancient healing cults?

Chapter Three

Christian Healing and Miracles

The miracles of Jesus presented in Luke and other parts of the New Testament confirm his involvement in the physical dimensions of the world and that he was truly incarnate in flesh and blood. His miracles were "signs" that the physical world was permeated by the divine power that could heal illness and drive out evil spirits. These miracles were not magical acts but rather symbolic actions that evoked a faith response in those who witnessed them.

We have examined the role of healing and the medical arts within the Greek culture prior to the birth of Christianity in the first century CE. Even though Jesus of Nazareth was clearly part of the Jewish culture and religious tradition, very soon after his death the Apostle Paul was able to transform the teachings of Jesus into a message that resonated within the Greek-speaking Gentile world of the first century. Spiritual and physical healing was very much part of the first century world in which many types of healers interacted with the more rational methods of the medical arts. Pliny the Elder (23 – 79 CE) "noted that the powers to heal or transform took both a natural (*ratio*) and super-natural (*religio*) form. The boundaries of magical belief in the Roman world were not clear and much of medical practice was supernaturally rooted."[1] In the New Testament we find over sixty occurrences in which Jesus performs some form of physical or spiritual healing. We also find twenty-four instances in which Jesus heals specific individuals.

In the New Testament era, the Israelites and other Near Eastern peoples did not have a unified concept of nature. They felt that most natural events were caused by the operation of a divine being or beings that controlled the natural and the supernatural world. The Israelites claimed to be monotheists although they were often attracted to other deities that were part of the cultural fabric of the Middle East and Near East. Many of these competing deities were reflections of the powerful forces found in nature that often seemed to be unpredictable and chaotic. They assumed that Yahweh had supreme control over any other deities and all natural forces in the universe, but this belief often wavered as we see in the story of the Israelite people wandering in the desert and worshipping a golden calf.

Most natural disasters were presumed to be the result of punishment for man's disobeying the divine will. The Hebraic concept of God's intervention in natural events had an element of uncertainty and unpredictability that stood at variance with the more ordered and systematic concepts of causality found in Aristotle and the Hippocratic Corpus. Hebrew had no word for "nature" or even for our western concept of "miracle" as a suspension of nature's physical laws. The focus of the Hebrew Bible's understanding of "miraculous works," such as the Exodus, was the saving power of Yahweh who intervenes to save the Israelite people and liberate them from their oppressors. The New Testament also reflects an understanding that nature is not governed by fixed principles of natural laws but rather by the power (*dynamis*) of the divine found in Jesus. Miracles are considered signs (*semeion*) of God's intervention in an event or a person's life. Since nature was not ordered or systematic, Jesus' powers of healing could not then be considered "miracles" in our modern sense of the word. The

New Testament concept closest to the word "miracle" is that of "power" or *dynamis*. Our English word "dynamic" originates from this Greek word. For the early Christians, the Incarnation of Jesus into human history represented the "power" or *dynamis* of God, taking the form of a human person who was and is the Son of God. God's power to save and to heal became manifest in Jesus. This same power is communicated to the Apostles at Pentecost and they, in turn, are able to share in this power to heal and to save others as Jesus did. The Gospel of Luke and the Book of Acts are generally attributed to Luke the physician, a companion and colleague of Paul mentioned in Col. 4:14 and 2 Tm 4:11. The Gospel of Luke was written for Gentile Christians and already shows Gentile (rather than Hellenistic) influence. The parables of the Lost Sheep and the Good Samaritan seem to refer to the idea that the salvation promised by the Good News extended to all men and women, not just the Jews. Although the historiography is clearly meant to show the universality of Jesus' message and ministry, the Gospel still fits well within the apostolic traditions about the birth, ministry, death and resurrection of Jesus. The universal claims that Luke presents in his Gospel reflect his desire to address the Gentile community of his time. The prologue to the Gospel is presented as an historical account of Jesus' background, beginning with his birth, and placing that birth in a specific cultural and geographical context. The universal claims that Luke presents in his Gospel reflect the Gentile community to which this Gospel is addressed.

The Acts of the Apostles starts with the scene from Pentecost when the Holy Spirit comes down upon the apostles and disciples of Jesus to form the first *ecclesia* or community of faith. The Acts of Apostles shows the *logos tou theou*, the word of God, spreading beyond its original environs of Jerusalem and its Jewish matrix to the center of the Roman Empire, where Paul preaches to the Jews in Rome. He tells his listeners, "Understand, then, that this salvation of God has been sent to the pagans; they will listen to it" (Acts, 28:28). In order to appeal to his audience, Luke also gives a more prominent role to women than was found within the Jewish communities of that time. In the Hellenistic world, women had more social and legal rights and privileges than was common among Jewish faith communities. In Luke's story of the woman who repents her sins, Jesus chides the Pharisee who invited him to the meal for his lack of compassion toward this woman of ill repute. Jesus states that "It is the man who is forgiven little who shows little love....But he said to the woman, 'your faith has saved you, go in peace'" (Luke 7:48 – 49). Another story highlighting Jesus as the friend of sinners is the classic story of the Prodigal Son (Luke, Ch. 15). Luke also presents the "miracle" stories of Jesus as expressions of the compassion of Jesus for those who are suffering.

Luke's Gospel also seems to function as a gentle critique of Gnostic-oriented Christians. *Gnosis* or enlightenment presumed that the initiate had already arrived at a spiritual state of being which transcended the material order. The Gnostics tended to believe that the resurrection and ascension of Jesus was the culmination of human history. Through baptism, the Gnostic could enter the resurrected state himself, thus arriving at a complete and final state of participation in the kingdom of God. Luke stresses, however, that the resurrection and ascension must be followed by the gifts of the Spirit so that the Gospel can be carried to the Gentile world. Some Christians also believed that the fall of Jerusalem was a sign of the end of human history. Luke states, however, that Gentile mission must first be accomplished before the end time could come.

In addition, the Gnostics had difficulty accepting the full humanity of Jesus. They were particularly troubled by his suffering, passion and death, which they felt to be beneath his divine nature. Some Gnostic Christians believed that the divine spirit had come into Jesus during the period of his earthly ministry but that it left the human Jesus before his passion and death. The Gnostic view was that a divine redeemer could not possibly submit himself to suffering, torture and death. Irenaeus confirms this view of the Gnostics in his writings *Against Heretics*.[2] Luke stresses that the Holy Spirit came into Jesus from the moment of his conception and remained through his ordeal on the cross. Luke has Jesus speak to God while on the cross, "Father, into your hands I commend my spirit" (Luke 23:34). Luke also shows that there were witnesses to Jesus' death. "And when all the people who had gathered for the spectacle saw what had happened, they went home beating their breasts"[3] (Luke 23:48). The miracles of Jesus presented in Luke and other parts of the New Testament confirm his involvement in the physical dimensions of the world and that he was truly incarnate in flesh and blood. His miracles were "signs" that the physical world was permeated by a divine power that could heal illness and drive out evil spirits. These miracles were not magical acts; rather, they were symbolic actions that evoked a faith response in those who witnessed them.

To what extent are the stories of Jesus' healing powers similar to those of the Asclepian tradition of Greece? Morton Kelsey's classic study, *Healing and Christianity*, claims that the "theological attitude of Jesus makes one of the basic differences between the healing of Jesus and those in other ancient cultures, particularly in the Greek world. The Greek god Aesculapius (Roman spelling) was simply one divine power among many, a god who happened to be interested in healing."[4] On the other hand, we might question a total separation of Jesus' healing ministry from other healing figures of the Hellenistic world. Luke's emphasis upon the healing ministry of Jesus might have resonated within his Gentile audience precisely because they had a prior understanding and acceptance of the healing power of the Greek god Asclepius.

Luke's story of the Transfiguration of Jesus contains symbolism that resonates with the Asclepian tradition of healing through awaking from sleep. In this story, Luke states, "Peter and his companions were heavy with sleep, but they kept awake and saw his glory" (Luke 9:32). For those Gentiles familiar with the Asclepian cult, Jesus represented a new type of healer who transforms the believer from the "sleep" of sin and death to the "glory" of the divine presence manifested in Jesus. Sleep was a metaphor in Greek culture for entering into another state of consciousness that awakened the devotee of the god Asclepius to the divine message. In Luke, we find a similar message that might resonate in the minds and hearts of his Gentile audience.

The author of Luke was familiar with the Gentile culture of that time and must have known about the Greek healing tradition. Jesus is presented as a healer who fits within that tradition but with much greater power than Asclepius. In Luke's story of the the widow of Nain, the widow's son is restored to life as a sign of God's compassion for the mother and her child. This "sign" of God's power leads the crowd to be "filled with awe and praised God saying, 'A great prophet has appeared among us; God has visited his people.' And this opinion of him spread throughout Judaea and all over the countryside" (Luke 7:16-17). It seems clear that Luke is emphasizing the *impact* of the "miracle" as much as the "miracle" itself. He is trying to show that the power of Jesus to heal is related to his universal message of salvation for all mankind and that the Gentiles were meant to benefit from this Good News.

We find a similar kind of power over natural phenomena in Chapter 8 of Luke when Jesus gets into a boat with his disciples. A storm arises while at sea and the disciples fear the storm will sink their boat, drowning them all. They awaken Jesus from sleep and plead with him to save them. "Then he woke up and rebuked the wind and the rough water; and they subsided and it was calm again. He said to them, 'Where is your faith?' They were awestruck and astonished and said to one another, 'Who can this be, that he gives orders even to wind and waves and they obey him?'" (Luke 8:25). Again, the emphasis is on the reaction of those who experience the power of Jesus to rebuke the wind and the waves. Miracle stories were common in the ancient world because they were understood "not as something contrary to natural laws, but as something that rouses admiration, that transcends ordinary human power, that is inexplicable for man, behind which another power—God's power or even an evil power—is concealed."[5]

We know from the archeological evidence at healing temples in Greece that cures of illness were common in the ancient world. Most of these "cures" were credited to some form of intervention by one of the gods or goddesses. We also know that shamans performed similar ceremonies to relieve various forms of illness within the Native American and indigenous religious traditions. Illness was considered an affliction of both body and soul in the ancient world. The modern idea of illness as primarily a physical malady would have been unthinkable for most ancient peoples. They felt that illness always had both mental and spiritual dimensions. However, modern medicine now acknowledges the role that the mind and emotions play in the onset of illness and the role that meditation and imagery can play in the healing process. These psychosomatic or behavioral factors indicate that the healing process is complex and relational in nature. Given the widespread belief in healing in the ancient world and the important role that healers played in many ancient cultures, it is quite understandable to view Jesus as part of this long tradition.

Jesus' healing actions were never done against a person's will. Those kinds of powers would be considered magical. He always exercised his power in the context of the faith of those who were healed. In the story of the Centurion's servant, Jesus indicates that it is the faith of the centurion that surpasses his reception by the people of Israel. "When Jesus heard these words he was astonished at him and, turning around, said to the crowd following him, 'I tell you, not even in Israel have I found faith like this.' And when the messengers got back to the house they found the servant in perfect health" (Luke 7:9-10).

Carl Jung claimed that physical healing was often intimately connected to the psychic healing that took place when a patient was able to gain access to the contents of his or her unconscious life. "Faith" can be seen in this context as an opening of the conscious mind to new symbolic material that is evoked in the presence of a healer such as Jesus. Jung felt that the unconscious contained both destructive elements as well as healing elements. In his *Memories, Dreams, Reflections*,[6] Jung discusses the "confrontation" with his unconscious and the types of fantasies that were released in his dream life. Morton Kelsey states, "In discussing dreams he (Jung) wrote that they often show 'a remarkable inner symbolical connection and a definite psychic problem,' so that in many cases it looks as if the physical disorders were directly mimicking the psychic condition."[7] Jung also states that images were important in transforming emotional states that he found threatening and possibly debilitating.

> To the extent that I managed to translate the emotions into images—that is to say, to find the images which were concealed in the emotions—I was inwardly calmed and reassured. Had I left those images hidden in the emotions, I might have been torn to pieces by them.... As a result of my experiment I learned how helpful it can be, from the therapeutic point of view, to find the particular images which lie behind the emotions.[8]

Jung uses the word "experiment" to describe the process by which he used his therapeutic skills to confront psychosomatic disorders that were partly psychic and partly physical in nature. Perhaps we can also claim that Jesus had the gift of a "medical intuitive" who could discern both the interior and exterior causes of a physical malady. His *dynamis* could be considered a kind of therapeutic understanding of the psychological contents of physical illness that lead to a sense of isolation and hopelessness. Jesus and other ancient healers were experts in discerning the images that could be used to help the ill person mobilize his or her own internal *dynamis* to become whole again. We do not need to presume a "magical" interpretation of these miracles if we utilize the insights gained in the twentieth century through the "science" of depth psychology. Jung was perhaps the first to fully understand how a person's interior life and unconscious can be the source of physical illness as well as physical and psychological healing. The miracle stories in which Jesus raises a person from death (such as the Lazarus story[9] [John 11:1-44]) or the young man at Nain (Luke 7:11-17) pose another set of questions.

Through the use of scientifically-based Form Criticism of the New Testament as found in the Jesus Seminar, we can claim that these stories are rooted in the belief of the early Christian community and that they do not have to be literal historical narratives. The authors of these stories wish to show that the risen Christ is Lord even over death itself. Similar stories of people rising from death were common in the ancient world and usually were meant to show the amazing power (*dynamis*) of the one who worked such a "miracle." The Gospel narratives reflect the early Christian belief that Christ had conquered death itself through his own resurrection. These stories were meant to educate and elucidate this belief for those who were members of the Christian faith community.

These narratives are retrospective in character and not contemporary eyewitness accounts. They presume faith in Christ on the part of the reader and that he or she wants a fuller understanding of this faith. In many cases the narratives are similar to Old Testament stories of the wondrous works of God, such as those found in the parallel between the Exodus redemption narrative and the redemptive narrative surrounding Christ's passion, death and resurrection. Jesus is portrayed as the New Moses who leads his people out of the desert of slavery to sin to the Promised Land of the New Jerusalem, where he reigns supreme with the Father over the forces of sin and death. They are more theological in substance and tone and not meant to be historical narratives.

The question of the uniqueness of the "miracle" stories found in the New Testament is another important theological question. Most apologists for Christianity have asserted that the cures were unique to the power of the resurrected Jesus and that he alone could work such cures. Hans Küng takes exception to this view by stating that

> ...the primitive Christian communities shared their contemporaries' enthusiasm for miracles and the possibility cannot be excluded that they transferred to Jesus *themes and material from outside Christianity*, in order to emphasize his greatness and authority. This

> sort of thing happened with all the great "founders of religions," whose fame was enhanced by miracle stories. At any rate, we cannot simply distinguish between the pagan and Jewish miracles on the one hand and New Testament miracles on the other by asserting that the latter are historical while the former are not. Votive tablets found at the shrine of Asclepius in Epidauros and at other sanctuaries attest to numerous cures and healing ascribed to Asclepius. Rabbinic and particularly Hellenistic miracle stories of cures, metamorphoses, expulsions of devils, raising the dead, calming the storms were circulating in abundance.[10] (Author's emphasis)

The healing actions of Jesus were not, then, completely unique in the historical context of his time. Jesus was a charismatic healer who attracted numerous people who were physically ill or suffering from mental afflictions. His actions

> ...cannot be shown to be without analogies in the history of religion. They cannot be ascribed uniquely, incomparably, unmistakably, to Jesus alone and to no other person. But they were astonishing at least to the people of his own time....More important than the number and extent of the cures, expulsions of devils and wonderful deeds is the fact that Jesus turns with sympathy and compassion to all those *to whom no one else turns*: the weak, sick, neglected, social rejects."[11] (Author's emphasis)

According to recent studies in medical anthropology, we should distinguish between the categories of "illness" and "disease." "Patients suffer 'illnesses,' physicians diagnose and treat 'diseases.' Illnesses are *experiences* of disvalued changes in states of being and in social function; diseases in the scientific paradigm of modern medicine, are *abnormalities* in the *structure* and *function* of body organs and systems.[12] By embracing lepers, women of ill repute, tax collectors and other people on or outside the boundary of Jewish society of that time, Jesus was primarily concerned with the cure of "illness" as a social stigma that was attached to certain physical, psychological or social conditions. John Dominic Crossan may overstate his case by seeming to rule out any cure of a "disease" in the "miracles" of Jesus and only a cure of "illness."

> This is the central problem of what Jesus was doing in his healing miracles. Was he curing the disease through an intervention in the physical world, or was he healing the illness through an intervention in the social world? I presume that Jesus, who did not and could not cure that disease or any other one, healed the poor man's illness by refusing to accept the disease's ritual uncleanness and social ostracization.[13]

Crossan rules out the charismatic effect that Jesus could have had on the ill person, which would account for many of the cures mentioned in the New Testament.

Given our contemporary understanding of the unity of the mind, body, and spirit, we cannot rule out that the charismatic influence of a healer such as Jesus could affect such a real cure. The person's "faith," however, played a central role in such a cure.

Most of the miracles found in the New Testament are primarily described as "signs" of God's constant healing power now present in Jesus through his post-resurrection state of being. They are not meant to be purely historical narratives. The act of the raising of Lazarus in John's Gospel is intended as a sign that all who believe in Christ will be raised from the dead as well (John: 11:1-26). Jesus seems to arrive too late to help, yet he states that "our friend Lazarus is resting, I am going to wake him" (v.11). Death is considered a temporary sleep and Jesus will awaken all believers.

Jesus accepts the reality of death, and he states his belief in eternal life. "If anyone believes in me, even though he dies he will live and whoever lives and believes in me will never die." The removal of the stone from the tomb of Lazarus symbolizes the removal of the sting of death for all who believe in Christ. All who believe in him are now "unbound" and "set free" from the bonds of death.

The "miracle" stories in the New Testament were generally written as invitations to believe in the Risen Christ. They are post-resurrection narratives with a specific intent to instill the same faith in the listener that is portrayed in the stories they recount. The New Testament was largely written many years after the events it narrates, including the miracle accounts. We can understand them as image-laden stories that helped the hearer to enter a mythological and symbolic world which was "real" to the hearer and helped them to transform their isolated and marginalized state of being into one of wholeness and inclusion in a new community of faith inspired by the teaching and ministry of Jesus. Within a Jungian and medical perspective, we might consider Jesus to be a "therapeutic" healer who could help those who were ill to mobilize their own inner powers and discover their natural wholeness as children of God. The discovery brought about by his charismatic presence could be a central component of the "miracle" which occurred. This does not rule out, however, a physical healing as well as a mental and spiritual recovery. The ancient world did not divide reality between these seemingly separate domains. They felt that all of life was composed of all three dimensions, physical, mental and spiritual, and that a healing act affected all three dimensions of a person's existence.

Recent anthropological studies on the "meaning" dimension of healing indicate that the healer is someone who can decode the cultural and social context of illness. The core meaning of *stigma* in Greek was "to mark or brand." The "sign" or "stigma" on their bodies physically identified slaves, criminals or other ostracized persons. Someone who was "stigmatized" was "branded" by society as possessing some evil spirit or condition that made them an outcast from the mainstream culture. According to Goffman, the stigmatized person internalized this external sign as a "spoiled identity, a feeling of being inferior, degraded, deviant and shamefully different."[14] This deviant person has broken cultural conventions and hence is feared by the dominant culture of his or her community. Arthur Kleinman states "A stigma often carries a religious significance—the affected person is viewed as sinful or evil—or a moral connotation of weakness and dishonor. Thus, the stigmatized person is defined as an alien other, upon whose persona is projected the attributes the group regards as opposite to the ones it values."[15]

Examples of this type of ostracism are found among lepers in India and AIDS patients in the United States. In China, mental illness has a similar cultural stigma that affects not only the mentally ill person but his or her entire family.[16] Jesus' healing powers may be understood as the *dynamis* to break the psychological and physical hold that these social and mental constrictions had on the ill person. His acceptance of them and his ability to confront and transform the conventional interpretation of their illness may have been an important part of his healing presence. Dr. Ira Progroff, noted for his development of the Intensive Journal program, states, "In earlier centuries and in simpler societies than ours, the task of healing was undertaken by means of special incantations, by rituals and prayers, and by focusing the energy and power of the individual who was felt to have healing qualities on the person who was ill. This was the vitalistic form of healing."[17] The other form of healing, according to Progoff, uses the "materialist medical" approach to healing. This approach is found today in the medical sciences influenced by discoveries in biology, chemistry and the use of various technological advances. When healing is brought about by the "materialist medical" approaches, the individual may not grasp the necessity to understand the personal meaning contained in the illness. If the "message" of the illness has not been absorbed into the person's consciousness, the illness may return in a more pronounced form. Progroff states, "It is one thing to identify the meaning of an illness by analyzing the 'causes' and proximate sources from which it seems to have come. It is something else to enter into a relationship with the illness by which the illness is able to articulate its message for the life."[18] Jesus must have been a holistic healer in the traditions of the ancient world since he helped the ill person to understand the meaning of his or her illness.

Faith and healing are conjoined in the New Testament stories that deal with Jesus' healing powers. Through faith, the individual was able to find the hidden meaning in his or her illness and relate to it in a new way, not as an ostracized, alienated and sick person, but as someone who was aware of a new dimension of his or her being that was now whole and complete. This transformation of consciousness could have occurred in the light of the clarity and charisma that Jesus brought to the ill person and his sense of how the patient needed to be healed. The Gospel stories that emphasize Jesus' power over death emphasize his presence as the Risen Christ who has conquered sin and death. They invite the reader or listener to become one with Christ and share in his victory over those forces that diminish or destroy our common identity and destiny.

---

[1] L.D. Hankoff, "Religious History in the First Century," *The Journal of Psychohistory* 19(4), (Spring, 1992).

[2] Irenaeus, Adversus Haereses I, vii, 2. Elaine Pagels, the noted scholar of early Christian Gnosticism, has shown that the views of Irenaeus were slanted against the Gnostics, and that he helped to define the orthodox essence of the Christian faith. Elaine Pagels, Beyond Belief (New York: Random House, 2003), 82 – 92.

[3] I am indebted to Joseph Grassi's study on Gnostic influences in early Christianity found in his *Underground Christians in the Earliest Church* (Santa Clara, CA: Diakonia Press, 1975), 82 – 92.

[4] Morton Kelsey, *Healing and Christianity*, (NY: Harper and Row, 1978), 59.

[5] Hans Küng, *On Being a Christian* (NY: Image, 1984), 228.

[6] Carl Jung, *Memories, Dreams, Reflections* (NY: Vintage, 1965), Chapter 6.
[7] Kelsey, *Healing and Christianity*, 292.

[8] Op. cit., 177.

[9] See the Jesus Seminar material on the New Testament, including writings by scholars such as John Dominic Crossan, Marcus Borg and John Shelby Spong at the Westar Institute web site: www.westarinstitute.org.

[10] Op. cit., 234 – 235.

[11] Ibid., 234 – 235.

[12] Leon Eisenberg, "Disease and Illness: Distinctions Between Professional and Popular Ideas of Sickness," *Culture, Medicine and Psychiatry* (1977), II.

[13] John Dominic Crossan, *Jesus: A Revolutionary Biography* (San Francisco: Harper, 1993), 82.

[14] Erving Goffman, *Stigma* (NY: Simon and Shuster, 1963), 3. Quoted in Arthur Kleinman, *The Illness Narrative* (New York: Basic Books, 1988).

[15] Ibid., 159.

[16] Ibid., 160.

[17] Ira Progroff, *Finding the Message of Illness* (NY: Dialogue House, 2003), 2.

[18] Ibid., 3.

Questions for Discussion

1) What was the view of Nature found in the time of Jesus and the writers of the New Testament?

2) What was the New Testament understanding of Jesus' miracles?

3) What is your own understanding of what constitutes a "miracle?"

4) What was the role of "faith" in the stories of Jesus' miracles?

5) What can the historical sciences tell us about the nature of the miracle stories found in the New Testament?

6) What are some alternative interpretations of the miracle stories that are based on modern psychology and anthropology?

Chapter Four

Greco-Roman Medicine, Christian Ethics and Islamic Medicine

Even though Galen was not attracted to Christianity, he is considered a monotheist who believed in a Creator God after the fashion of the Platonic Demiurge. According to Galen, Nature was an expression of the divine purpose and nothing the Creator made was accidental or chaotic. Nature reflected a perfect design of the Creator's rational purpose and the rational "soul" was the closest expression to the imprint of the Creator.

In the Roman world of the late first and early second centuries, four schools of medicine emerged and were competing with each other for patients. The "Rationalists" or "Dogmatists" were somewhat united in their desire to practice theoretical medicine based on the principles of natural philosophy. They relied upon physiological theories that had emerged from Hellenistic medicine and the Hippocratic Corpus. The "Empiricists" were opposed to theoretical assumptions about disease or illness, including the search for physiological causes of disease. They were also opposed to human dissection as unnecessary and harmful. They felt that any therapy should be based on past experience and the practical outcomes that resulted from traditional medical treatments. A third group of physicians, called the "Methodists," arose around the first century CE in Rome. They claimed that both the "Rationalists" and "Empiricists" had made medicine too complicated and that many forms of disease were caused by stresses on the body that could be cured through bringing the body back into its natural balance. This form of medicine is similar to the holistic or behavioral approach now becoming popular in many parts of the United States, which also draws upon eastern forms of spirituality. A fourth school, that of the Pneumatists, was based in the principles of Stoic philosophy. They believed that the macro-cosmic world was composed of a world-pneuma (spirit) which all living beings share and which was manifested in the breath. They focused on an analysis of a patient's breath as a key to their health or sickness.

Galen, the most famous physician in the ancient world after Hippocrates, was born in Pergamum in 129 CE, on the Agaedian coast of modern Turkey. Pergamum was a Greek-speaking colony of the Roman Empire at this time. Galen's father, Aelius Nicon, was a prominent architect and builder who had an enthusiastic interest in mathematics, astronomy and logic. At a young age, Galen became an "attendant" at the temple of Ascelpius in Pergamum (attendants assisted visitors to the temple and prepared them for the healing rites overseen by the temple priests). This sanctuary of Asclepius was considered one of the most important cultural and healing centers for the Roman province of Asia. Initially, Galen's father guided his son's education toward philosophical and scientific pursuits. When Galen was seventeen years old, however, his father had a dream in which Asclepius urged him to direct Galen toward the vocation of medicine. Galen's first medical studies, with a focus on anatomy, took place at the sanctuary of Ascelpius. After his father's death, Galen moved to Smyrna and went on to the great medical training center at Alexandria. Galen returned to Pergamum in 157 and became physician to the gladiators, a very prestigious position for a young doctor. Galen became well-known for his understanding of the anatomy of the human body. He performed many dissections and vivisections on animals and some human dissections which increased his understanding of anatomical and physiological functions. Galen accepted the basic Hippocratic understanding of the four humors constituting the central functions of the human body: blood, phlegm, yellow bile and black bile. In the time of Galen, the cause of disease was primarily considered to be an imbalance in the humeral system as first proposed in the Hippocratic Corpus. Galen furthered medical understanding by investigating the role of specific organs in various types of diseases. He also wrote extensively on the importance of "reading" a patient's pulse and examining his or her urine as part of medical diagnostic procedures. In his *Anatomical Procedures*, Galen "supplied excellent descriptions of the bones, the muscles, the brain and nervous system, the eyes, the veins and arteries and the heart."[1] Galen's understanding of anatomy was conveyed to Europe through Islamic interpreters and became the standard interpretation of anatomy until the Renaissance. Following the thought of Plato that human beings had a threefold division of the soul into the rational, animal and vegetative functions, Galen developed his own interpretation of these functions. For Galen, the brain was the seat of the soul's rational functioning and the source of the nerves in the body; the heart was the seat of the "passions" and source of the arteries. Galen had a theory of vital spirit or "pneuma" which flowed out to the whole body from the heart, and he considered innate heat as the life-giving force that was generated within the heart. The lungs served as a kind of "bellows" for the heart to produce innate heat or to moderate it; the lungs and respiration helped to maintain the right balance of heat in the body. The liver was the seat of desire or "appetite" and the source of the veins, which enable the venous blood to flow through the body.

Galen's physiology was founded upon his understanding of Aristotelian philosophy, that every part of the body had its own particular purpose which could be interconnected with other systems in the body. He found evidence of intelligent design in every aspect of human and animal anatomy and physiology. Even though Galen was not attracted to Christianity, he is considered a monotheist who believed in a Creator God after the fashion of the Platonic Demiurge. According to Galen, Nature was an expression of the divine purpose and nothing the Creator made was accidental or chaotic. Nature reflected the perfect design of the Creator's rational purpose and the rational "soul" was the clearest expression to the imprint of the Creator. The "argument for design" for the existence of God and his benevolent providence over creation became a standard philosophical concept in the later medieval period. Galen's linking of Aristotelian teleology with his own medical empiricism made him the standard-bearer of medical understanding until the Renaissance era. Islamic authors, such as Avicenna, would modify and improve upon Galen's physiology and anatomy. His underlying medical philosophy, however, remained largely intact as it came back into the West via Salerno in the eleventh century through the translations of Galen's works by Constantine the African. Galen left Pergamum for Rome about 161 CE. He soon became the most influential physician in Rome and was eventually made physician to the imperial court of Marcus Aurelius. Galen's public lectures and his writings became central to the growth of his reputation. He was one of the most prolific authors of the ancient world and rivaled Aristotle for the scope and depth of his scientific and philosophical writing. We have over eighty extant works by Galen, containing a blend of medical, philosophical and philological analysis. Galen often engaged in debate with other physicians and considered his own methods and philosophy far superior to those of the three schools that were common before his ascendancy. The Roman aristocracy agreed. Also, Galen did not reject the role of astronomy in understanding the forces that would affect human equilibrium. As late as 1833, editions of Galen's Greek works (Karl-Gottlob Kuhn's edition) were still considered valuable resources for medical professionals and classical scholars.

Galen accepted the importance of dreams in making a diagnosis of a patient's illness. He wrote a treatise, entitled

On Diagnosis in Dreams, in which he distinguished between ordinary dreams that were affected by the balance or imbalance of the humors in the body, and "prophetic" dreams. But since in sleep the soul does not produce impressions based on dispositions of the body only, but also from things habitually done by us day by day, and some from what we have thought—*and indeed some things are revealed by it in a fashion of prophecy* (for even this is witnessed by experience)—the diagnosis of the body from the visions-in-sleep (*enhypnion*) that arise from the body becomes difficult.[2] (Author's emphasis).

Galen admits that the "visions-in-sleep" are relevant to the examination of the patient, and he shows that the "vision" may be related to the humeral balance or imbalance in the patient. The "prophetic" dreams, he states, are more difficult to classify, and the presumption is that these types of dreams may be related to some kind of celestial message.

Now if it were necessary only to distinguish this cause from the things done or thought by day, it would not be at all difficult to conclude that whatever has not been done or thought is arising from the body. But since we concede that there are also prophetic dreams, it is not easy to say how these might be distinguished from the ones arising from the body."[3]

Galen seems to take the position of an agnostic as to the source of these dreams. He does not, however rule out some form of divine message such as was common in the Asclepian dream tradition of Greece. We know that Galen did not believe that miracles were possible because he felt such a belief would contravene his strong Aristotelian belief in the orderly structure of Nature. A miracle would be a kind of lapse in the divine ordering of the universe, which did not seem intellectually compatible with Galen's natural philosophy.

The naturalistic world of Galen's medical philosophy would later stand in contrast to the nominalistic views of William of Ockham in the later medieval period. According to Ockham, God was free to intervene at any point in the process of creation and change his will or his purpose. God was sovereign over all, including the ability to bring about a healing miracle or allow a disease to run its course. The concept of a "faith healing" becomes more possible within the Occasionalist philosophy of Ockham, but it also led to a separation of the natural and supernatural forms of healing.

The British Museum has an exhibit on Roman medicine. It contains an item which depicts, in a small ring, a Roman physician examining the abdomen of a young boy while the god Asclepius looks on. The ring is dated from the first or second century CE, very close to the period in which Galen had his medical career. This ring exemplifies the continuing connection in Roman medicine between the "scientific" and "spiritual" dimensions that informed Roman medical practice during this era. Even though we can find no evidence of Christian faith within the Galenic corpus, it does seem clear that he had a spiritual understanding of the human psyche because of his recognition of dream states as revelatory of deeper causes of illness, and that access to some kind of power beyond the normal rational investigation that he generally espoused was needed. We can assume, then, that Galen emphasized the scientific aspect of medicine but that he remained open to the "spiritual" aspects of dreams for their prophetic character. Since he had begun his medical career at the sanctuary of Asclepius, we can presume that he retained some reliance upon the kinds of healing powers that might be released through the "vision-in-sleep." Galen's belief in an ordered universe seemed to rule out miraculous interventions of the gods but he seemed to have some realization that archetypal powers were released in dream states that were difficult to classify within the scientific categories of his time. It may be that this is a bridge between the healing traditions of the New Testament era and the medical traditions that we find in the Roman Empire in the second century CE.

The medical profession was limited to men from the Roman era through the Renaissance. The growth of the male priesthood within the Roman Catholic Church after the fourth century can be compared to the development of the medical profession in Europe during the Middle Ages. In the later Middle Ages, theological studies and training in the medical arts were often intermingled with the training of candidates for the priesthood. Since the earliest Christian times, Christ had been described by many of the early Christian writers as the *Christus Medicus*[4] or the "divine physician." The Fathers of the early Church also utilized medical analogies to describe Christ's ministry.[5]

We surmise, then, that in the ancient and medieval world, the demarcation line between the healing arts and the medical arts was often blurred. Most physicians relied upon a mixture of practical wisdom and the medical "science" of that time as well as "referrals" to the healing cults that seemed to always be a part of popular culture. Just as we have the use (and possible abuse) of alternative healing modalities in the contemporary world, so, too, we can find many instances of such examples in the ancient and medieval world. The difference, however, would be that in the Roman and early Christian eras, very few people had access to more learned medicine. Most of the populace had to rely upon "healers" who often combined indigenous healing crafts with elements of superstition, magic and some degree of wisdom about the human psyche and the value of herbal remedies.

We now know that the medical "science" of the ancient world was largely limited to the physiological discoveries of Galen and even these were limited in scope. The Hippocratic tradition presumed that the natural healing powers of the body could alleviate most illnesses and that the physician's role was largely confined to helping to restore balance in the patient's bodily systems. Galen took this tradition further by his acute observations about the anatomy and physiology of the body and his ability to determine how the various bodily systems were interconnected and interdependent. He also continued the Aristotelian assertions that each bodily function was purposeful and part of a larger teleology that informed both the human body and all of Nature. The divine purpose found in Nature was illustrated by the rationality found in the human soul, which directed bodily functions through its seat in the brain.

Galen made substantial advances in the practice of medicine through his emphasis on meticulous observation of the body's anatomy and physiology. He did not identify with any of the previous schools of medicine but, instead, he incorporated both rational and empirical approaches to examining symptoms, seeking natural causes and cures for specific ailments. He also believed in keeping detailed records and wrote an immense number of volumes on medicine, philosophy and philology. We still have record of over eighty of these texts but he may have written as many as 300 volumes. He frequently criticized his contemporaries for their lack of rigor and used his skill in rhetoric to debate his opponents.[6] He felt that many of his opponents were relying on pure speculation and that they did not have an empirical basis for their assertions. He relied heavily on the Hippocratic tradition in regard to the four humors and he developed his own theories, such as the central role of the pulse in determining a person's temperament. The four elements of the universe, (earth, air, fire and water) corresponded to the four personality types: melancholic (earth), choleric (fire), sanguine (air) and phlegmatic (water). The four humors, (black bile, yellow bile, blood and phlegm) corresponded to the four elements.

Galen believed that illness was the result of improper anatomical functioning, which could be linked to particular organs of the body. Hippocrates also believed that illness implied some bodily imbalance in the four humors but he did not localize this imbalance to particular organs. Galen was also interested in the movement of the blood through the body although he did not discover how the blood actually circulated. He was able, however, to distinguish the difference between veins and arteries. He knew that the veins and arteries carried blood through the body but he did not understand the role of the heart in pumping blood. His experiments and anatomical investigations led to the discovery of many nerves in the body, including several cranial nerves. He believed that the body functioned with three distinct systems and that each was essential for the life of the person. The "animal spirit" was found in the brain and it was responsible for sensation and thought; the "vital spirit" was located in the heart and symbolized life energy; the "natural spirit" was found in the liver and the veins and was responsible for nutrition and growth. Galen's three-fold distinction about the location of the operational centers of the human body, also known as the rational, animal and vegetative souls, were first identified within the thought of Aristotle. This "hierarchy" of souls would later appeal to the Church authorities of the Middle Ages, who essentially "canonized" Galen as the preferred authority on medical theory. Galen's Aristotelian teleology also seemed to support the rational foundation for all aspects of human biology, which appealed to the medieval understanding that the whole universe was "designed" in the mind of God. Galen's influence in the West was mediated by the Islamic world in that many of his texts were lost in the early Middle Ages and only reappeared in the twelfth and thirteenth centuries by way of Arab commentators or translations from Arabic texts of his numerous works.

The New Testament teachings on healing based on faith in Christ and the Roman understanding of medicine developed along parallel yet interdependent tracks in the Middle Ages. In a study on the legacy of the Hippocratic Oath during the early Middle Ages, Carlos R. Galvao-Sobrinho shows how the Hippocratic medical tradition began to merge with the early medieval Christian culture.[7] St. Jerome, the author of the Latin Vulgate edition of the Bible, wrote an intriguing letter to a recently-ordained priest who had sought him out for advice. Jerome tells the young priest

It is your duty to visit the ill, to be acquainted with the households, the matrons, their children, and the secrets of noble men. Let it also be your duty to keep chaste eyes, and a chaste tongue. May you never speak of the looks of women, and may never any household know of the secrets of another through you. *Hippocrates made his disciples take an oath* before he taught them, and compelled them to swear by his word. He demanded that they keep silence, and he described for them their speech and posture, their dress and manners."[8] (Author's emphasis).

Even though some of the items mentioned by Jerome are not found in any extant editions of the Hippocratic Oath, the main purpose of Jerome's remarks are clear. He is invoking an "ancient authority" to encourage the young priest to live up to ideals similar to those customary for the medical profession. We find here a close affinity between the medical profession and the Christian priesthood.

We find in Jerome's letter an ethical ideal that was supposed to govern both the work of the priest and that of the physician. In effect, they were bound by the same type of moral code, including the classical oath of secrecy regarding "privileged matters" brought to either the priest or the physician. Jerome has either taken liberties with the Oath or he is presenting an evolved understanding of the Oath within the Christian culture of his time. It is clear, however, that on the level of ethics and priestly and medical etiquette, the priest and physician are following a very similar set of moral guidelines. Jerome was one of the most respected authorities within the Western Church and his views held great authority.

In the early Christian era, we can see a shift in understanding about the role of the physician in society. Because of the lack of formal training and theoretical knowledge for physicians, the emphasis in many of the early medieval documents was not so much about the level of theoretical knowledge they may have had about medicine or theology, but rather "about issues of morality, deportment, and appearance, bearing directly on their professional relationship with patients."[9] In the ancient world, physicians did not think of ethics in terms of personal attributes but, as we have seen embodied in the Galenic philosophical foundation for medicine, as impersonal and abstract principles. In the Middle Ages, we see a movement away from these abstract principles and an emphasis upon the physician's character. "Setting out to define what kind of a person the physician should be, not how he should behave, medical treatises placed the physician's personal qualities at the center of a discussion about medical ethics."[10]

We can see that the Christian faith was beginning to influence the medical profession in that the medical profession was taking on many of the moral characteristics presumed to govern the life of the priest. From the very early period of Christianity, care for the sick and dying was considered an important dimension of the Christian faith.

> Early Christian literature is full of admonitions to care for the sick. Although concern for the ill was urged upon all Christians in the early church, it increasingly became the specific duty of deacons and deaconesses to report cases of sickness or poverty to the local bishop. After the legalization of Christianity, bishops acquired a civic status similar to that of important government officials and assumed the responsibility of managing large-scale charitable efforts.[11]

Shortly after the legalization of Christianity in the fourth century CE, we find evidence of early Christian hospitals (*xenodochia*) in the eastern portion of the Roman Empire. These institutions began to be erected within a generation or two after Christianity became legal. One of the earliest, and probably the best-known, was the Basilea, which was founded in about 372 by Basil the Great (329 – 379), Bishop of Caesarea in Cappadocia. Basil provided accommodations for travelers, as well, and apparently the institution had a section for the treatment of lepers. The hospital had both nurses and medical attendants. Gregory of Nazianzus (333 – 389), who had seen the Basilea, described it in enthusiastic terms.

> Go forth a little from the city, and behold the new city, the treasure house of godliness, in which disease is investigated and sympathy proved. We have no longer to

> look on the fearful and pitiable sight of men like corpses before death, with the greater part of their limbs dead (from leprosy), driven from cities, from dwellings, from public places, from water-courses....Basil it was more than anyone who persuaded those who are men not to scorn men, not to dishonor Christ their head by their inhumanity towards human beings."[12]

Basil's hospital became a model for many others that spread throughout the eastern Roman Empire and later into the West. Non-Christians recognized hospitals as uniquely Christian organizations that were often linked with hospitality houses that served orphans, the aged and infirm and the poor.

Christians initially seemed to put more emphasis on the spiritual healing that took place through the laying on of hands or by the sacramental ministries of the church. The Eucharist was soon viewed as a healing remedy. Casesarius of Arles (470 – 543) stated: "Let him who is sick receive the body and blood of Christ, and then let him anoint his body."[13] As Christians began to establish more and more hospitals, they began to employ physicians in these hospitals. Basil expressed the Christian understanding of how the "medical art" could glorify God.

> We must take great care to employ this medical art, if it should be necessary, not as making it wholly accountable for our state of health or illness, but as redounding to the glory of God....In the event that medicine should fail to help, we should not place all hope for the relief of our distress in this art....We should neither repudiate this art altogether nor does it behoove us to repose all our confidence in it....When reason allows, we call in the doctor, but we do not leave off hoping in God.[14]

With the decline of established civil and educational institutions in the West after the fourth century, miraculous healing cults, along with practices that had a magical character, began to grow in popularity. After the legalization of Christianity in the fourth century, ascetics, monks and other holy men and women strove to replace the fervor of the early religious period characterized by persecution and martyrdom with extreme forms of ascetical practices. The cult of relics became very popular, particularly those associated with holy men and women who were martyred for their faith during the Roman persecution. Other saintly figures were revered and their tombs often became places of pilgrimage. St. Augustine was initially skeptical of miraculous reports, but he did take up an interest in them and in the healing power of relics at the end of his life. Several of these stories can be found in the last book of his *City of God*.[15] We know that the Rule of St. Benedict emphasized care for the sick as one of the fundamental Christian duties: "Care of the sick must rank above and before all else, so that they may truly be served as Christ, for he said: *I was sick and you visited me....*"[16]

"The *xenodochia* that survived the chaos of the disintegration of the Carolingian Empire usually became the property of monasteries. In the early Middle Ages, monasteries were also places of refuge for the poor and the sick."[17] Some of the monasteries had very skilled *medici* (doctors) in residence. However, most of their training occurred through internships and lacked, for the most part, any formal or academic preparation. Some of the great Carolingian monasteries did have some Greek medical texts that had been translated into Latin. These included some of Galen's writings, medical *Aphorisms* and other texts dealing with dietetics, *material medica* (drugs), phlebotomy and bathing. The key monasteries that possessed these texts were Corbie, Reichenau and St.Gall.[18] The transformation of the medical profession would occur in the eleventh century at Salerno, where we find the first examples of a systematic study of academic medical materials in the West. The founding monastery of the Benedictine order, Monte Cassino, in southern Italy, would play a crucial role in the reintroduction of classical Greek medical knowledge into the West. Under the direction of Abbot Desiderius, who later became Pope Victor II, the abbey of Monte Cassino became home to the noted translator of key Arabic medical texts, Constantine the African. Constantine had traveled extensively throughout the Middle East and was a convert to Christianity from Islam. Constantine and his monastic pupil, Johannes, were the key conduits for the translation of the *Pantegni* of Haly Abbas, the *Viaticum* of Abu Djafar, the treatises on fever and urine by Isaac Judaeus, Galen's *Tegni* and the *Aphorisms* of Hippocrates. "All of these treatises were to form the backbone of medical instruction for a long time at Salerno as well as elsewhere."[19]

The medical school at Salerno was the first example of organized medical instruction to occur in Europe and was in evidence by the end of the tenth century. Constantine and his pupil, Johannes, were not teaching at Salerno but their translations soon became part of the key medical knowledge taught there. As Kristeller states, "In any way, after the middle of the twelfth century the translations of Constantine become the common property of the Salerno school and even the center of its medical teaching."[20] Constantine's translations were important because they helped to reintroduce Greek natural philosophy into the medical school curriculum. "Perhaps more important for the long run for European medicine were the translations Constantine made of Arabic authors—treatises on diet, fever and urines by Isaac Israeli, and the *Pantegni* of Haly Abbas."[21]

Constantine seems to have been convinced of the connection between medicine and philosophy; the latter works have a strong theoretical and philosophical orientation, new in medieval Europe, which came eventually to mark Salernitan medicine.[22] The *Pantegni* is divided into two ten-chapter sections, the first dealing with the theoretical principles of medicine and the second with the practical application of theoretical principles. Even though Constantine probably did not complete the translation of the whole document, his influence is felt throughout it. The second part of the *Pantegni* is usually attributed to his pupil, Johannes Afflicius.[23]

Stephen of Antioch later translated the *Pantegni* or *Kitab al-Maliki* in 1127 under the title of *Regalis dispositio*. (The *Pantegni* was also known as the *Royal*

Art of Medicine, hence the title *Regalis dispositio*). Paul Oscar Kristeller, noted authority on the early history of the University Salerno, states

> Constantine's writings had a very considerable effect upon twelfth-century Salerno (as the core of the collection entitled *Ars Medicine* or *Articella* which was the foundation of much European medical instruction well into the Renaissance, they exerted a more diffuse influence for centuries)....It (Constantine's writings) did not merely enlarge the sphere of practical competence of the Salernitan physicians; it also had the added effect of stimulating them to try to organize the new material into a wider, philosophical framework.[24]

Kristeller's general claim of Arabic influence upon western medicine is supported by another authoritative history of medicine from Oxford University Press.

> Just as early Greek medical teaching served as a common intellectual framework for professional medical practice in the Islamic Near East, so Arabic medical literature of the ninth to twelfth centuries, through Latin translations, provided late medieval Europe with ideas and practices from which early modern medicine eventually arose.[25]

The practice of Arabic medicine in the early Middle Ages was truly an ecumenical endeavor, since the leading figures in the profession of medicine came from Jewish, Christian and Islamic backgrounds. Arabic was the common language of scientific philosophy and medicine, but non-Muslim physicians spoke or read many languages, including Greek, Syriac, Hebrew, and Persian. Some of the medical knowledge within the Islamic culture actually came from India via Sanskrit medical texts. These texts were translated in modern-day Persia during the Sassanid era and then traveled to Baghdad during the Abbasid caliphate in the ninth century. "The medical profession in general transcended the barriers of religion, language and country. Consequently, in this context, the term Islamic culture or Islamic medicine is not to be interpreted as applying only to the religion of Islam."[26] We can claim, therefore, that Islamic medicine contributed in a subtle way to the growth of an academic science of medicine that was not limited to any particular set of religious beliefs. Islamic medicine did, however, draw much of its inspiration from the Prophet Muhammad's understanding of human nature. "The Prophet provided the foundation for a medical tradition that considered a human being in his totality; the spiritual, the psychological and the physical were considered within the context of a social milieu."[27] Even though the Islamic medical tradition was greatly influenced by the religious principles found in the Prophet's teaching, it relied primarily on its assimilation of the Greek medical tradition as mediated through Galen the physician of Greco-Roman origin in the second century CE. Islamic medicine relied on "Galenic anatomy and physiology and Galenic theories of health, disease (including epidemic disease), diagnosis and therapy. An important aspect of Galenic influence was the linkage it revealed between medicine and philosophy."[28] Avicenna's *Canon of Medicine* would become the standard interpretation of this holistic theory of medicine until well into the Renaissance. The three great encyclopedias of Islamic medicine were the *Almanzor* of Rhazes (al-Razi, d. ca. 930); the *Pantegni* of Haly Abbas (d. ca. 904); the *Canon of Medicine* by Avicenna (Ibn-Sina, 980 – 1037). In addition to Constantine the African, Gerard of Cremona (ca. 1114 – 1187) was the other great translator of Arabic medical thought into Latin. Gerard did most of his translating work in the Toledo, and his contributions included numerous treatises of Galen that were extant only in the Islamic world until his translations of the *Almanzor* of Rhazes and the *Canon of Medicine* by Avicenna. He was also responsible for the first translation into Latin of a portion of the encyclopedia of surgery, *At-Tasrif (De Cirugia, "surgery")* by Albucasis (Al-Zahrawi, 936 – 1083) of Cordoba.

The treatise by Albucasis became the major influence on the practice of surgery in the Latin West until late in the Renaissance. It contained numerous illustrations of surgical instruments that were transmitted to the West through this text.[29]

Another authority on the history of early medieval science, David Lindberg, states

> These new texts vastly broadened and deepened western medical knowledge giving it a much more philosophical orientation than it had possessed during the early Middle Ages and ultimately shaping the form and content of medical instruction in the newly founded universities."[30]

As Kristeller notes, the term *medicus* was commonly used to denote the identity of the doctor in the prior period of Roman and earlier medieval history. After about the year 1100, we find the term *physicus* used for the name of the doctor, from which we derive the English word "physician." This shift in terminology seems to imply, according to Kristeller, a shift in focus toward natural philosophy within the medical training of the doctor. "(The) term *physicus* for doctor occurs in the documents from the early twelfth century on."[31] Kristeller notes that the study of the relationship between medicine and philosophy during this formative period still remains as a task for the scholars of this unique period in the history of Arabic and western European medical thought and practice.

The interaction between Greek natural philosophy and the medical profession would continue to characterize much of scientific development over the period of the twelfth and thirteenth centuries. It did not, however, curtail the growth of the moral and spiritual ideals that seemed to be implicit in the medical profession, as we have seen from our earlier examination of the early Christian understanding of medical ethics and etiquette. In addition to Greek natural philosophy, we find many of the innovations and scientific discoveries that characterized Islamic medical practice, plus many of the discoveries, theories and techniques, entered into the medical education of western physicians beginning at Salerno in the twelfth century, and then spread to other centers of medical education in Europe. Both Islamic and Christian medieval medicine was influenced by astrology. It was common to consult the stars before prescribing a particular medical treatment. The ancient world associated the heavens with various forms of divine influence. Even within Greek philosophical literature, we find support for ideas associated with astrology. In Plato's *Timaeus*, we find that the Demiurge assigns to the planetary deities the functions of ordering and bringing into existence the sublunary realm. Aristotle gave the "Unmoved Mover" the power to initiate movement in the lower terrestrial region. The Stoics also identified the microcosmic world of human and earthly life with the macrocosmic realm of the planetary universe. Many Islamic medical doctors were also astrologers. Abu-Nasr ('Adnan ibn-Nasr al-Aynzaarbi, d. 1153), personal physician to the Fatimid caliph in Cairo, discusses the astrological knowledge which is necessary for a medical doctor.

> After he had by way of introduction referred to the saying of Hippocrates already mentioned ("the science of the stars performs no small service to medical science, indeed an extremely large one"), he explained that the individual planets in certain positions prognosticate certain illnesses. The doctor must utilize the knowledge of these things for diagnostic and prognostic purposes. Especially in the case of bleeding, the stellar constellation must be observed.[32]

Ptolemy, considered the greatest authority on astronomy in the ancient world, wrote an astrological handbook, the *Tetrabiblos*, which was widely circulated in the ancient and medieval worlds. Ullmann states, "However, by and large, astrological considerations play only a small part in Arabic medicine. Whereas in the West, unfavourable conjunctions of the planets were constantly considered to be one of the chief causes of plague."[33] Other authorities claim, however, that ancient authorities such as Ptolemy "exercised a powerful influence on both the Islamic and Western astrological traditions."[34] The opposition to astrological theories within both the Islamic and Christian West was not, according to David Lindberg, "the belief in celestial influences, but the threat of determinism and (among the church fathers) the assignment of divinity to the stars and planets."[35] Philosophical and theological considerations played important roles throughout the medieval period in all aspects of the emerging scientific culture, including that of medicine. It is difficult, if not impossible, to separate academic medicine in this period from other influences that permeated both Islamic and Christian cultures. Both of these cultures were attempting to reconcile natural science as understood primarily within the Greek philosophical traditions, although augmented by the Galenic medical philosophy that drew heavily from Aristotelian thought. It is necessary to clarify how the philosophical teachings of Plato, Neoplatonism and Aristotelian thought influenced both Galenic medicine and its absorption and interpretation in the Islamic world of the eighth, ninth and tenth centuries.

We must further understand how the Galenic tradition may have been modified or expanded within the Islamic culture prior to its transmission to the West. It is clear that many of the great Islamic philosophers were also medical doctors or wrote medical texts. Among these are the two greatest philosophical luminaries of the Islamic world, Avicenna and Averroes. Kristeller notes that "Arabic influence, scholastic method, philosophy and astrology were definitely linked with scientific progress, at least for a specific period."[36] Further study is required to clarify precisely how these influences impacted the emerging medical education as it was first understood at Salerno, influences which then moved on to other centers of medical education at the universities of Montpellier, Paris, and Bologna. Kristeller notes that the leading centers of medical education in the thirteenth century probably received the curriculum that was first established at Salerno in the late eleventh and twelfth centuries.

The emergence of an academic medical curriculum seems to parallel the development of a professional medical class in many urban centers of Europe, as well as the decline of medical practice among the clergy and monasteries. As Lindberg states

> The driving force behind those developments (of academic medicine) was not mere intellectual curiosity or medical altruism (though a measure of both no doubt existed), but the desire for status and professional advancement. Physicians already at the top of the medical hierarchy outlined above, and therefore already literate, perceived the possibility of elevating their status by imitating other learned professions, such as law, in demanding that practitioners acquire formal intellectual credentials.[37]

The establishment of medical education within the universities cannot be separated from the introduction of Islamic philosophy and natural science that entered these same universities in the latter part of the twelfth and thirteenth centuries. Following the absorption of this new medical curriculum into the medieval universities, largely influenced and composed of Arabic medical texts translated into Latin, medical knowledge linked with other branches of the arts and sciences to become an integrated and systematic academic enterprise, rather than a craft supported only by on-the-job training and minimal academic study. Lindberg states again, "It also gave medicine access to Aristotelian natural principles, which would provide medicine with some of its important principles, and to astrological theory (and its companion, astronomy), which would become a universal part of the physician's diagnostic and therapeutic armory."[38]

[1] David C. Lindberg, *The Beginnings of Western Science* (Chicago: University of Chicago Press, 1992), 127. For the relationship of ancient philosophy to Greek medicine, see Ludwig Edelstein's "The Relation of Ancient Philosophy to Medicine," *Bulletin of the History of Medicine* 26 (1952): 299 – 326. For background on Galen in his historical context, see "Galen in the Eyes of his Contemporaries," *Bulletin of the History of Medicine* 58 (1984): 315 – 324. See also *Galen on Anatomical Procedures*, Charles Singer, ed., (Oxford: Oxford University Press, 1999). The earliest work of Galen available to us is *Galen on Medical Experience*, Dr. R. Walzer, ed., (Oxford: Oxford University Press, 1944).

[2] *Galen, On Diagnosis in Dreams*, translated by Lee T. Pearcy. See www.ea.pvt.k12.pa.us/medant/dedign.htm

[3] Ibid.

[4] R. Arbesmann, "The Concept of 'Christus Medicus' in St.Augustine," *Traditio* (1954), 10: 4 – 5.

[5] D.W. Amundsen and G.B. Ferguson, "Medicine and Religion: Early Christianity Through the Middle Ages," in *Health, Medicine and the Faith Tradition*, eds. M.E. Marty and K.L.Vaux (Philadelphia, 1982), 93 – 131.

[6] See Tasmyn Barton's excellent study on the role of rhetoric in Galen's teaching found in *Power and Knowledge: Astrology, Physiognomics and Medicine Under the Roman Empire*, (Ann Arbor: University of Michigan Press, 1994).

[7] Carlos R. Galvao-Sobrinho, "Hippocratic Ideals, Medical Ethics, and the Practice of Medicine in the Early Middle Ages: The Legacy of the Hippocratic Oath," *Journal of the History of Medicine and Allied Sciences vol. 51* (1996): 439 – 455.

[8] Ibid., 440 – 441.

[9] Ibid., 446.

[10] Ibid., 448.

[11] D. W. Amundsen and G. B. Ferngren, "The Early Christian Tradition" in R.L. Numbers and D.W. Amundsen, eds., *Caring and Curing: Health and Medicine in the Western Religious Traditions* (New York, NY: Macmillan 1986), 48.

[12] Ibid., 49.

[13] Ibid., 52.
[14] Ibid., 52.

[15] City of God, 22.8.

[16] T. Fry, ed., *The Rule of St. Benedict in English, St. Benedict, Regula 36.1* (Collegeville, MN: Liturgical Press, 1982), 59.

[17] *Caring and Curing, op.cit.*, "The Medieval Catholic Tradition." Darrel W. Amundsen. p.83.

[18] "History of Medicine" in the *Dictionary of the Middle Ages, vol.8.* (NY: Scribners, 1987), 247.

[19] Paul Oscar Kristeller, "The School of Salerno," in *Studies in Renaissance Thought and Letters,* (Roma: Edizione Di Storia E Letteratura, 1956), ch. 24, 510. For an historical study of the Monte Cassino monastery, including the period under Abbot Desiderius, see William M. Johnston, ed., *Encyclopedia of Monasticism,* vol.2, (Chicago: Fitzroy Dearborn, 2000), 883 – 885.

[20] Ibid., 511.

[21] The Pentegni in its Latin translation can be found in *Migne Patrologia Latina.* CL (Paris, 1880), cols, 1559 – 1566. See also Charles Burnett's *Constantine the African: The Pantegni and Related Texts* (Leiden: Brill, 1994). The French authority on the introduction of Arabic science into the Latin West is Danielle Jacaquart; see *La Médicine Arabe et L'occident Médiéval* (Paris: Maisonneuve-et-Larose, 1989). See also Lynn Thorndyke's treatment of Constantine the African in *The History of Magic and Experimental Science* (New York: Columbia University Press, 1963), ch. 32. Also important is *H. Schipperges, Die Assimilation der arabischen Medizin durch das lateinishche Mittelater* (Wiesbaden, 1964). For an important general summary of the transmission of Arabic medicine into the Latin West, see Nancy G. Siraisi's *Medieval and Early Renaissance Medicine: An Introduction to Knowledge and Practice* (Chicago, University of Chicago Press, 1990). Michael Ullman's *Islamic Medicine* is the standard general history of Islamic medicine (Edinburgh: University of Edinburgh Press, 1978, reprinted 1997). A more recent study, but more limited in focus, is Michael Dols', *Medieval Islamic Medicine: Ibn Ridwan's Treatise "On the Presentation of Bodily Ills in Egypt"* (Berkeley: University of California, 1984). See also Michael Dols' article "The Origins of the Islamic Hospital: Myth or Reality," *Bulletin of the History of Medicine* (1987): 367 – 390.

[22] "History of Medicine" in *The Dictionary of the Middle Ages,* vol.8 (NY: Scribners, 1987), 248.

[23] Op.cit., 393.

[24] Op.cit., 394.

[25] Irvine Loudon, ed., *Western Medicine: An Illustrated History* (Oxford: Oxford University Press, 1997).

[26] Ibid., 40. The philosopher/medical doctor Rhazes or Razi (ca. 854 – 925) was skeptical of any authority figure in philosophy, religion or medicine. He can be considered one of the first religious and medical "skeptics." "The miracles supposed to have been worked by the prophets of the three monotheistic religions as well as Mani were tricks." Razi viewed medicine as a philosophy capable of change and development. "Medicine is a philosophy, and this is not compatible with renouncement of criticism with regard to the leading (authors such as Galen)." *Dictionary of Scientific Biography,* vol. XI, 323.

[27] Mansour Solyman Al-Said, "Medicine in Islam," in *Encyclopedia of the History of Science, Technology and Medicine in Non-Western Cultures.* (London: Kluver Academic Publishers, 1997), 696.

[28] Ibid., 324. Manfred Ullmann, author of the standard work, *Islamic Medicine*, states "Of all the Greek doctors, Galen was for the Arabs by far the most significant. It could not be otherwise for, since the third century, Galen's medicine had been completely dominant in the east of the Hellenistic world. By the second half of the ninth century nearly all Galen's works had been translated into Arabic." Manfred Ullmann, *Islamic Medicine* (Edinburgh: Edinburgh University Press, 1978), 10.

[29] Richard Lemay, in *Supplement I of the Dictionary of Scientific Biography*, presents a detailed discussion of the medical texts (24) translated by Gerard of Cremona. A shorter summary of *Gerard of Cremona* by Richard LeMay is found in the *Dictionary of the Middle Ages*, vol. 5, 422 – 423. See also the important work by Loren MacKinney, *Medical Illustrations in Medieval Manuscripts* (London, Wellcome Historical Medical Library, 1965). For an English translation of *De Cirugia* by Abulcasis, see M.S. Pink and G.L. Lewis, *Albucasis on Surgery and Instruments: A Definitive Edition of the Arabic Text with English Translation and Commentary* (London: Publications of the Wellcome Institute of the History of Medicine, 1973). The latter work also contains illustrations of the surgical instruments found in *De Cirugia*. Another work translated by Gerard exists in English translation: A. Altmann and S.M. Stern, *Isaac Israeli, a Neoplatonic Philosopher of the Early Tenth Century* (London, Oxford University Press, 1958). This work contains a translation of the *De Elementis* and the *Liber difnitionum* of Ishaq al-Israilli (Isaac Israeli).

[30] Op. cit., 327.

[31] Ibid., 515.

[32] Manfred Ullmann, *Islamic Medicine* (Edinburgh: Edinburgh University Press, 1978), 112.

[33] Ibid., 114.

[34] Lindberg, op.cit., 275.

[35] Lindberg, op.cit., 277.

[36] Kristeller. op.cit., 512.

[37] Op. cit., 330.

[38] Op. cit., 330.

Discussion Questions

1) Discuss the importance of Galen in the historical evolution of medical knowledge in the ancient world.

2) How did Islam and Christianity view ancient medical knowledge?

3) What is "medical philosophy" in the light of ancient and medieval thought?

4) How did Greek medical knowledge become part of the Islamic and Christian cultures of the Middle Ages?

5) What role did Salerno play as the first Western "medical school?"

Chapter Five

Gnosticism, Hellenism and Christianity

Matthew Fox notes that Teilhard de Chardin,
the evolutionary mystic of the twentieth century,
emphasized the theme of the Cosmic Christ to
justify his own evolutionary cosmology.

Christianity was born within a Jewish matrix, but soon it left the stable in Bethlehem for the long journey to the centers of the Greco-Roman world, Rome and Alexandria. The Apostle Paul was a Roman citizen who translated the messianic vision of the early Jewish community of faith into a Hellenistic Christian cosmology that appealed to the universality of the Greek and Roman mind. After the death of Jesus, the messianic revolutionary currents within Judaism, led by the Zealot movement, continued to grow. It reached a critical threshold around in year 70 CE, when the Jews revolted against the Roman rule in Palestine. In the war that followed, the rebellion was forcibly crushed and the Jewish Temple was destroyed. The Christian community was dispersed from Palestine, as well, and moved out into the Gentile world. Hellenistic culture and the Roman Empire and its laws were both cosmopolitan in character. The prior Alexandrian empire and the present Roman Empire provided a kind of archetype for a more universal civilization that could serve the spread of the Christian message.

Paul's theology and cosmology found expression in his early epistles to Greek-speaking converts living throughout the Roman Empire. Paul claimed that Christ had not only transformed the redemptive order of personal salvation, but the entire order of Nature through his death and resurrection. Paul tended to contrast the wisdom of Greek philosophy of an ordered and rational cosmos with the "wisdom" of the crucified Christ.

> Do you see how God has shown up the foolishness of human wisdom? If it was God's wisdom that human wisdom should not know God, it was because God wanted to save those who have faith through the foolishness of the message that we preach. And so, while the Jews demand miracles and the Greeks look for wisdom, here are we preaching a crucified Christ (I Corinthians 1:21 – 23).

Even though Paul seems to impugn Greek philosophy, he is, in fact, very concerned that he present a Christian cosmology that would make sense to his Greek converts. Paul's theology of creation envisages Christ as the New Adam brought about by his death and resurrection, resulting in a new creation. "And so for anyone who is in Christ, there is a new creation, the old creation has gone" (II Corinthians 2:1 – 3). The Genesis account, according to Paul, is replaced by the new creation story found in his cosmological vision of the Cosmic Christ.

Paul does not disparage the created order as the Gnostics would tend to do in the second century of the Christian era. In his letter to the Ephesians, Paul explains in more detail the cosmological implications of the new creation wrought by Christ and how it fits into the divine plan. According to Paul, God wished to place all of creation under the influence of Christ. "He (God) had let us know the mystery of his purpose, the hidden plan he so kindly made in Christ from the beginning to act upon when the times had run their course to the end; that he would bring everything under Christ, as head, everything in the heavens and everything on earth" (Ephesians 1:9 – 10). The letter of Paul to the Philippians includes a hymn to the Cosmic Christ in which Christ is considered an exalted ruler in the heavens.

> Who, though he was in the form of God,
> did not count equality with God
> a thing to be grasped,
> but emptied himself,
> taking the form of a servant
> being born in the likeness of humanity.
> And being found in human form
> He humbled himself and became obedient unto death
> Even death on a cross.
> Therefore, God has highly exalted him
> And bestowed on him the name
> Which is above every name,
> That at the name of Jesus
> Every knee should bow
> In heaven and earth and under the earth,
> And every tongue confess that Jesus Christ is Lord,
> To the glory of God the Creator (Phillipians 2:6 – 11).

This probable early Christian liturgical hymn reflected the cosmology of the early Christian era, with its emphasis on the lordship of Christ over the whole known universe.

> The early Christians who sang this hymn are employing
> the cosmology of the Hellenistic world of their time,
> the threefold division of the universe into heaven, earth
> and the under-the-earth realm....Schillebeeckx (a noted
> Catholic theologian), commenting on this passage, says
> "the striking thing is that this lordship of Christ is not

related to the community of the church of God, as is almost exclusively the case in Paul, but to the universe."[1]

Matthew Fox notes that Teilhard de Chardin, the evolutionary mystic of the twentieth century, utilized the theme of the Cosmic Christ to justify his own evolutionary cosmology and called the Cosmic Christ the "third nature" of Christ, "meaning that it takes us beyond the fourth-century councilor definitions of Christ's human and divine natures into a third realm, 'neither human nor divine, but cosmic.'"[2]

Paul developed a comprehensive understanding of the natural order transformed in the new creation wrought by the Christ event. We see not so much a Jesus of history as a universal cosmic personalizing force that informs both heaven and earth. Christ is that new unifying force field that holds together the fullness (*pleroma*) of the universe. He (Christ) reigns supreme over the impersonal and cosmic powers which were competing with him in the ancient view of the universe. Some of these principalities and powers seemed to overwhelm any human effort and were considered part of the "fate" that could entrap individuals or societies.

Paul asserted that the Cosmic Christ now had control over these forces, and that none of them could separate the believer from Christ. Shortly after the death of Paul, we find that Gnostic influences affected the teachings of the Christian faith. We have already discussed Gnostic influences in Luke's Gospel. In addition, Elaine Pagels discusses the influence of the Gnostic Gospel of Thomas on John's Gospel in her recent book, *Beyond Belief*.[3] Pagels shows that early Christianity was much more diverse than traditionally thought and that Gnosticism appealed to many parts of the Hellenistic and Latin- speaking world. Some of the Gnostic teachers, such as Valentinus and Ptolemy (not the cosmologist Ptolemy who will be treated later), relied on prophetic revelations and dreams much like the popular Asclepian cult of healing. "Although they called themselves spiritual Christians, Irenaeus regarded them as dangerously deviant."[4] This conflict with Gnosticism would provide a strong impetus for the "rationalizing" of the Christian faith through an emphasis on tradition, the episcopacy and the canon of Scripture expressed in the Four Gospels and Paul's letters. Marcion (ca. 80 – 155 CE), one of the most noted second-century Gnostic teachers, established his own church organization and his own canon of Scripture. He felt that Christianity and Christ brought about a complete break with Judaism.

Most of what we know about Marcion comes to us through the writings of Tertullian. In his writings, Tertullian claims that Marcion distinguished between an inferior Creator God (akin to the Demiurge of Plato) and the God of the New Testament. The Old Testament God was responsible for allowing Adam and Eve to fall into sin and is thus inferior to the God of the New Testament, who brought the ministry of Christ the Redeemer into the world (*cosmos*). This form of dualism regarding the nature of the divinity helped to explain the problem of evil within a good created order. Marcion claimed that Jesus did not assume a material body because the material world was part of the evil cosmos created by the Old Testament God. In order to join the Marcionites, converts had to renounce sex and marriage. They also avoided meat and wine as part of their discipline.

Marcion's canon included only an edited version of Luke's Gospel and the ten letters of Paul. The Old Testament was not part of the Marcionite scriptural canon. Many of the early Church Fathers felt compelled to write refutations of Marcion because his ideas and his church organization spread throughout the Middle East, African and Europe. The oldest inscription from any Christian house of worship comes from Marcionite village in Lebanon. The inscription reads: "Place of worship (*synagoge*) of the Lord and Saviour Jesus Christ of the Marcionites in the village of Lebanon."[5] Marcion's popularity seems to be related to his simplistic explanation of the origins of evil in the world and a clear separation between the material and spiritual realms.

The Canon of the New Testament, as developed during the episcopate of Irenaeus in the latter second century, seems to have been in direct response to the Marcionite Canon. The emerging doctrine of the Incarnation which united matter and spirit in the person of Christ can also be viewed, in part, as a response to the challenge posed by Marcion.

The goodness of the created order was challenged again by the Manichean heresy in the fourth century. Its most noted critic was St. Augustine, the most important and influential of all the Latin Church Fathers; ironically, his initial conversion to a spiritual life was within the Manichaean tradition. The Manichaean teachings contained elements from Eastern and Western religious sources such as Babylonian (Middle East), Hindu (India), Zoroastrian (Persia) and both Judaism and Christianity. Manichaeism taught that there were two uncreated principles of Light (goodness) and Darkness (evil). Creation is the result of the interaction of these two principles. The Father of Light and the Prince of Darkness are doing battle in the created world. A follower of the Manichaean spirituality sought to liberate the elements of Light within by moral purification, good works and abstinence from sexual contact. Some elements of Manichaean spirituality can be found in Augustine's thought despite his rejection of the key tenets of dualism. Augustine's teaching on creation, original sin, the soul and the body would dominate the Western intellectual tradition for almost 800 years. In addition, his influence on the separation of Western psychology from cosmology would later appear in a new form with Descartes in the seventeenth century.

The first-century world of Paul was under the influence of sophisticated astrological systems that blended a view of the heavens as "home" of the gods and a predictor of earthly events. Astrologers attempted to use the latest astronomical techniques to determine the exact position of the planets at a person's birth, and to then show how this date in the planetary spheres coincided with the identities and actions of the gods and goddesses who resided in the heavens.

Ptolemy (aka Claudius Ptolemaeus), the greatest of the astronomers in the ancient world, lived in Alexandria from approximately 87 – 150 CE. He was an astronomer, mathematician and geographer. His geocentric view of the universe helped to systematize the apparent motions of the planets as they were understood at the time. His system involved at least eighty epicycles to explain the motions of the Sun, the Moon and of the five known planets. His system of ordering the motion of the planets around the Earth was called the Ptolemaic system. In this system, the outermost sphere of the fixed stars was presumed to travel westward around the Earth. Within that sphere, however, the Sun and Moon revolved eastward (at a slower rate) in a large circle called a deferent. The movements of other planets in smaller circles were called epicycles. Astronomers would adjust the rates of revolution of each deferent and epicycle to account for the variable movements of the planets. Ptolemy utilized even more sophisticated geometrical concepts, such as eccentrics and equants, to explain the variable movement and brightness of the planets and stars. The Ptolemaic system modified the Aristotelian geocentric vision of the universe but it did so without challenging the basic premise of the system that presumed an earth-centered universe. He also followed Aristotelian philosophy in claiming that astronomy is of a higher order of being because it is closer to the celestial realm of the Prime Mover. Ptolemaic cosmology would govern the West's scientific understanding of the universe for the next 1500 years.[6]

Ptolemy's book, *Mathematical Syntaxis* (commonly known as the *Almagest*), contained the most advanced mathematical understanding of the heavens found in the ancient world; and his influence continued until the time of Copernicus. Ptolemy also wrote an influential astrological treatise, called the *Tetrabiblos*, a kind of handbook for astrologers.

Astrological divination was utilized in the practice of medicine in the ancient world. It was believed that heavenly bodies influenced certain physical conditions. The astrologer claimed to understand how to determine this influence and make adjustments for it, if necessary, to improve a patient's health. The roots of astrology seem to originate in ancient Babylon. Berossos, a priest from Babylon, is supposed to have left Babylon for Ionia around 280 BCE and founded an astrological school on the island of Cos, where Hippocrates and his successors practiced their medical arts. The art of divination seemed to have some commonality with philosophy since Plato and Aristotle held that the stars were divine by nature. St. Augustine, in his *City of God*, warned against astrologers for they seemed to deny freedom of the will. He did believe that the stars had an influence on human actions, however, but that this influence would not compel our human faculties. As Christianity gained in favor, it repressed the influence of the astrologers. Christian philosophers and theologians did, however, attempt to incorporate many elements of Hellenistic thought into their theological views.

About the middle of the second century CE, we discover the first Christian intellectuals beginning a dialogue with the major philosophical schools of the ancient world. Most of these efforts were apologetical in tone; hence the name "apologists" for this group of thinkers. At this point in time, Christianity was considered an irrational superstition by many who were steeped in the Greek or Roman philosophical traditions. St. Justin Martyr (ca. 100 – ca. 165) was a pagan truth-seeker who explored the philosophical schools of Stoicism, Aristotelianism, Pythagoreanism and Platonism. Around 130 CE, he converted to Christianity and later opened his own school in Ephesus. After a brief period in Ephesus, he moved to Rome where he opened another school and wrote his *First Apology* about 155 CE. This work was addressed to the Emperor Antoninus Pius and his sons, Marcus Aurelius and Lucius Verus. His *Second Apology* was written after 160 CE and was addressed to the Roman Senate. Justin was attacked by the Cynic philosopher Crescens, and was later scourged and beheaded for refusing to sacrifice to the emperor.

Justin was the first Christian intellectual to attempt to reconcile the claims of faith and reason. He was not an original thinker, but he held that elements of the truth could be found in the pagan philosophers of antiquity.

He claimed that all human beings shared in the "germinative word" (*logos spermatikos*) which is a kind of "natural revelation." For Justin, the rationale for the Incarnation was founded on the need for Jesus to teach men their true nature as Sons of God. Based on his Platonist orientation, Justin held to a subordinate doctrinal position regarding Christ's human nature. Justin attempted to show that reason could lead one to faith and then support one's faith. Christ was the reason (*Logos*) in whom the whole human nature found its ultimate foundation, and those who lived according to reason were "seminal" Christians. Enlightened Greek philosophers such as Socrates, Plato and Heraclitus were considered such "seminal Christians" by Justin.

Irenaeus (ca. 130 – 200 CE), Bishop of Lyons, wrote his famous treatise *Against all Heresies* (*Adversus omnes Haereses*) sometime between 180 and his death. It was an important dogmatic and apologetic tract written principally to refute the claims of the Gnostics, who believed that only a select group of Christians were truly spiritual and were thus called the *pneumatkoi* or the "knowers of secret knowledge." This knowledge came to the Gnostics either by way of a special revelation or an unknown oral tradition handed on only to them from the Apostles. They generally believed that the origin of the material world came from the work of a Demiurge, similar in form to the thought of Plato in the *Timaeus*.

As we have discussed earlier, the Gnostic Demiurge was derived from an inferior Supreme Being, but did not share the perfection of even this being. This "Creator God" (a parallel with the Old Testament era) was the immediate source of creation and ruled the world. The material universe was, therefore, an imperfect and lesser form of being than that of the Supreme Being. According to Gnostic teachings, Christ had come as the emissary of the true Supreme Being to give certain men the divine *gnosis* which would free them of the restraints of the material world. As a divine being, Christ could not assume a human body or die, because this would be contrary to his divine nature. Christ could, however, act temporally through the human being, Jesus, to announce his Gnostic message to the world. Irenaeus did not try to oppose the Gnostic teachings on philosophical grounds, but rather through an appeal to the written tradition found in the four Gospels and the handing on of that tradition from the time of the Apostles. He even went so far as to list the names of the bishops of Rome to show the unbroken succession of leaders from the time of Peter and Paul to Eleutherius, the Bishop of Rome at the time Irenaeus was writing his famous treatise. Irenaeus may have overly simplified Gnostic teaching to show a clear demarcation point between the rather amorphous Gnostic tradition and the canon of the four Gospels. The four Gospels and the episcopal authority became a touchstone for Christian orthodoxy, in contrast to the more mythological doctrinal content of the Gnostics. In this process, the Gospel of Thomas became identified with Gnosticism even though it had extensive support from many groups within the early Christian era. Irenaeus is usually considered the first significant Catholic theologian. In opposition to the Gnostics, he held firmly to the unity of the human and divine in Christ. His doctrine of recapitulation (*anakephalalosia*, or summary of human evolution in the Incarnate Word), became an important new insight into the meaning of the Incarnation. The Word of God had existed from all eternity with God the Father and in the appointed time, the Word was made flesh in Jesus. Through his Incarnation, Christ became the Second Adam, summing up in his manhood the whole historical experience of the human race. The Incarnation brought about the union of God and man and the restoration of paradise for all mankind. Irenaeus emphasized the traditional elements of Church teaching, including the Canon of Scripture, the historic episcopate and the theological traditions dating back to the apostles. Irenaeus' traditionalist assault upon Gnosticism led to the destruction of the Gnostic Gospels. These Gospels were rediscovered around 1945 at Nag Hammadi in Upper Egypt. The documents were translations from Greek originals of works probably dating back to at least 140 CE. They included the *Gospel of Thomas*, the *Gospel of Truth*, the *Apocryphon (Secret Book) of John*, the *Gospel of Philip*, the *Gospel* of the Egyptians, the *Apocalypse of Paul*, the *Letter of Peter to Philip* and the *Apocalypse of Peter*. The campaign of Irenaeus against the Gnostics indicates that they were a very powerful movement in the second century and that they reflected a different understanding of the Christian life that many scholars now identify with "eastern" religions. By the time of Constantine and the First Ecumenical Council at Nicaea in 325, the traditionalist view of Christianity found in Irenaeus' writings had triumphed with the political support of the Roman Emperor.

These texts indicate that the Gnostics taught that an *interior* type of knowing, which today we might call *insight* or *intuitive* knowledge, was superior to purely *rational* knowledge. Through this type of *gnosis*, the disciple would attain the same identification with the divine that Jesus had. This type of knowledge bears a great similarity to the Buddhist understanding of "enlightenment." In the Gnostic *Testimony of Truth*, we find the story of the Garden of Eden found in Genesis but with a much different interpretation of the serpent. In this document, the serpent appears as the principle of divine wisdom and teaches Adam and Eve how to access the sources of this divine knowledge. The "Lord" is threatened by this action and banishes them from the Garden of Eden for attempting to be "equal" to the "Lord." Another text found in this same document is attributed to a feminine divine power that seems to be in opposition to the traditional image of the male transcendent deity

> For I am the first and the last. I am the honored one
>   and the scorned one.
> I am the whore and the holy one.
> I am the wife and the virgin....
> I am the barren one, and many are her sons....
> I am the silence that is incomprehensible....
> I am the utterance of my name.[7]

We know that the Gnostics had many prominent female teachers in the second century of the Christian era and that they posed a grave threat to the episcopal version of the Christian revelation. The Gnostic approach to Jesus does not require the same type of institutional mediation and legitimacy that we find in the more authoritarian version espoused by Irenaeus. The *Gospel of Thomas* views the teachings of Jesus as therapeutic in that they stress the need for the disciple to find his or her own interior strength of spirit. Both acknowledge the need for guidance, but only as a provisional measure. The purpose of accepting authority is to learn to outgrow it. According to the *Gospel of Thomas*, Jesus refused to validate the experience that the disciples should discover for themselves. "They said to him, 'Tell us who you are so that we may believe in you.' He said to them, 'You read the face of the sky and of the earth, but you have not recognized the one who is before you, and you do not know how to read this moment.'"[8]

The Gnostic approach to evil was not so much as moral evil, but the limitations posed in our human condition that led eventually to various forms of suffering and death. The psychological dimensions of suffering were also considered part of the "evil" (*kakia*) found in the physical universe. In order to escape from the "rootlessness" (*aporia*) of our temporal condition, the Gnostics taught that we needed to discover our interior nature that, in Jungian terminology, we might call the "higher self" or the "archetypal self." We can see that this form of knowledge is quite different from the "scientific" forms of knowledge developed within the philosophical context of the Hellenistic world.

Clement of Alexandria (ca. 150 – ca. 215) was the first Christian theologian to systematically explore the relationship between Greek philosophy and Christian revelation. Alexandria was one of the great centers of philosophical and theological speculation by the end of the second century, and was home to one of the most significant attempts to harmonize the world of Greek philosophy with the Christian message. Throughout the period of Roman domination, as a center of learning, Alexandria had both a major library and a museum. Many scholars, including those who commented on the works of Ptolemy, were attracted to these intellectual centers.

Writing about the year 200, Clement spoke of philosophy as a schoolmaster or pedagogue to bring the Greek mind to Christ, just as the law had been a tutor unto Christ for the Hebrew people. Hence, Clement was more sympathetic toward the Gnostic's search for religious knowledge than Irenaeus had been. Clement stated that the Church was the gathering of the elect, the pious and righteous Gnostics who taught and did God's will. Christ was the Logos, the source of all human knowledge and the bearer of God's divine knowledge to humankind. The Logos became man to reveal the mystery of God's being and invite man to share in that being through faith. The true Gnostic would rest on God's holy mountain, the Church on high. Here, these philosophers of God would be assembled with the saints to give themselves over to the pure intuition of God's infinite being. Clement was attempting to present the Christian Gospel to the educated classes of Alexandria

The Alexandrian school of theology was heavily influenced by Platonic speculation and tended to emphasize the divinity of the eternal Logos over his humanity. Clement founded this school of theology, but he was succeeded by his brilliant and controversial student, Origen (ca. 185 – ca. 254). Origen had studied Platonic philosophy under the tutelage of the noted Alexandrian Platonist, Ammonius Sacca. During a time of Christian persecution around 202, Clement had to flee from Alexandria; Origen was later appointed his successor. Origen became embroiled in a dispute between the bishop of Alexandria, Demetrius, and the bishop of Caesarea who later ordained him to the priesthood. He took refuge in Caesarea around 231, and established a catechetical school there. He continued his writing and teaching in Caesarea until his death.[9]

Origen was the Church's first great biblical theologian; he did important work in systematic theology, as well. His chief work of biblical criticism was the *Hexapla*, an arrangement of the Old Testament into six parallel columns with each column giving a different Greek translation of the text. Saint Jerome, the author of the Latin *Vulgate* version of the Bible (which later became the standard text of the Bible throughout the Middle Ages), would use Origen's edition for his own translation of the Scriptures. Origen also wrote numerous commentaries on the Bible as well as many homilies on specific texts. He utilized three viewpoints in his biblical interpretation: literal, moral and allegorical. He preferred the latter. The literal and moral views would be accessible to the common person, but allegory would only be understood by a mature believer.

Perhaps Origen's most famous doctrinal position was that of *apocotastasis*, which asserted that all living creatures with free will, (human beings, angels and even the devil), would be saved at the end of time after a final purification. This teaching ran counter to Christian orthodoxy but seemed to be compatible with the Platonic view of the material world as simply a shadow of the spiritual world, existing independently of any moral choice. Origen also believed in the immortality of the soul and the eternity of the created universe, a theory which was also held by Aristotle and Averroes and became the subject of much debate in the later Middle Ages. His emphasis on the allegorical sense is important; it shows that by the early second century, Christian theologians acknowledged that a literal reading of the Bible was not the only true interpretation that would be considered orthodox. The "science" of biblical interpretation would become one of the most important functions of theologians throughout the Middle Ages. This laid a foundation for interpretation of other religious and philosophical texts. The study of variations in biblical texts became part of the next task in biblical theology undertaken by St. Jerome (ca. 342 – 420).

Jerome was one of the great scholars of the Patristic era, and had mastered both Hebrew and Greek. About 386, he set out for Palestine where he established a monastery and devoted himself to the study of biblical manuscripts in their original languages. Early Christians had adopted the Greek Septuagint version of the Hebrew Scriptures and most lacked knowledge of the Old Testament in any other version. The New Testament was, of course, also written in Greek but survived in a variety of manuscripts. The Canon of the Scriptures had evolved over the first three centuries of the Christian era. However, Jerome's edition, called the _Vulgate_ or "common" version, became the standard for the next 1000 years. The Gutenberg Bible, the first printed book in the fifteenth century, was essentially the same document that Jerome had written approximately ten centuries earlier.

We find many paintings of Jerome throughout the Middle Ages in which he is pictured as a hermit in the desert with a lion at his feet. Jerome's initial biblical work was probably at the request of Pope Damasus, bishop of Rome from 366 – 384. Damasus asked Jerome to edit a new and more authentic text of the four Latin Gospels. The "Old Latin" version of the Bible had many inconsistencies, and Damasus was anxious to have these inconsistencies corrected.

Jerome probably completed his work on the Gospels shortly before the death of Damasus. He would later continue his work in Palestine and there he assembled one of the greatest manuscript collections of ancient versions of the Bible, including the _Hexapla_ of Origen. Jerome worked painstakingly to determine the most accurate and most consistent variation of the text, and he wrote extensive commentaries on the final Latin version. His use of the Hebrew manuscripts for the Old Testament superseded the _Septuagint_ version in Greek.

Jerome spent approximately thirty years on this project, and its significance cannot be underestimated. Jerome set the standard for methodology in historical and biblical studies that still is relevant today. Jerome did not have an understanding of the historical critical method of literary analysis that became part of nineteenth and twentieth century biblical scholarship, but he did have a scholar's sense of the importance of remaining true to the original biblical languages and the historical and social contexts in which they were written. Contemporary historical scholarship and historiography bear some degree of debt to the scholarship of Origen and Jerome.[10]

St. Augustine (354 – 430) was born in the small town of Hippo in North Africa (now part of Algeria). In his youth, Augustine was a student of Plato and Neoplatonism. For a period of about ten years, he was a follower of Manichean doctrine, which held to a dualistic understanding of matter and spirit. As we already noted, the Manicheans believed that there were two worlds, the world of goodness and light created by God and a world of evil and darkness created by the devil. In his youth, Augustine lived with a mistress and had a son named Adeodatus. In 383, Augustine left North Africa for Milan, where he met the Bishop of Milan, St. Ambrose. Augustine was greatly influenced by Ambrose, and in 387, Augustine was baptized into the Christian faith.

Augustine's early writings were heavily influenced by Neoplatonism. In *On Ideas*, Augustine presented his own theory of the Platonic Ideas. According to Augustine, the Ideas existed in the mind of God and have no existence outside of this. These Ideas are communicated to human beings through direct illumination by God. Augustine also wrote a treatise entitled *On True Religion*, in which he argued that philosophers who accepted the teachings of Plotinus regarding the One, the Mind and the World Soul would find greater clarity in the Christian doctrine of the Trinity, since this doctrine had many similarities to Plotinus' teachings.

Plotinus (205 – 270) was a pupil of Ammonius Sacca in Alexandria. Plotinus rejected Gnostic dualism, and he rejected the necessity of salvation because he believed there was a natural mystical ascending order of being. At the summit of being was the One. The next level of reality below the One is Mind (*Nous*). Mind looks downward toward Nature and creates the material world. The created world is the result of successive "emanations" from the One. The "World Soul" in the Plotinian universe is the intermediary between the physical world and the immaterial world of Ideas. In the spiritual world of Plotinus, each individual has the natural capacity to live a life of contemplation similar to that found in the eternal world of the Mind in its relationship with the One. This concept of contemplation would also have a great effect upon

St. Augustine. He felt, however, that only the Christian could truly know the higher spiritual realms and that Original Sin remained an insuperable obstacle to access to the divine Mind. The Plotinian and Augustinian emphasis on the duality of subject and object would later influence the theories of Grosseteste and Bacon in the thirteenth century and Martin Luther in the sixteenth century, and would bear some similarity to the thought of Descartes in the seventeenth century.

Augustine's most famous writing was his *Confessions* (ca. 400). In this treatise, he developed a very sophisticated theory of time that resonates with the twentieth century philosophy of science. Augustine held that prior to the creation of the universe, there was no time. Within God, there was no succession of past, present and future, but only an eternal present. He asserted that even within human history only the present is real; the past is only a memory and the future does not yet exist, since only the present has any reality.[11] Stephen Hawkings' *A Brief History of Time* is the classic study of time in the philosophy of science.[12] It is interesting to note that Hawkings gives credit to Augustine for clarifying the idea that in God there could be no succession of past, present and future. Hawkings also shows that time and space are intimately related in the General Theory of Relativity. Augustine's analysis of time and eternity was very subtle and exceeded prior attempts to understand how a Creator God would not compromise his eternity by entering into the world of Time. He would not become temporal and subject himself to the conditions of the temporal order. Augustine held that all of God's "actions" in the created order were a participation in the eternal realm of God's Ideas, akin to the Neoplatonic doctrine of a World Soul in which all intelligibility could be found and transmitted to the earthly plane.

Augustine defended the Christian doctrine of creation against the Manicheans. The Manicheans held that there was an eternal evil power opposed to God. Augustine claimed that all of the created order was good and that moral evil was a "privation" of goodness, rather than evil in and of itself. The Donatist controversy led Augustine to deal with questions about the validity of sacramental acts versus their regularity or legality in the eyes of the Church authorities. The relationship of the Church to the civil order was discussed at length in his *City of God*. It was written from about 413 to 426. The occasion for his writing the *City of God* was the fall of Rome to Alaric, one of the invading barbarian chieftains, about the year 410. This event signaled the collapse of the Roman Empire in the West. Some pagan Romans claimed that the fall was due to the abolition of pagan worship after Constantine converted to Christianity in 312 and imposed Christianity as the new religion of the Roman Empire.

Constantine's decision to move the capital of the empire from Rome to Byzantium (later called Constantinople) in 330 led to a power vacuum and growing dissolution of the Roman governmental structures that had ruled for centuries. Augustine distinguished the City of God as the idealized final state of human affairs, when God and Christ have penetrated and transformed all of human history. Meanwhile, during the interim between the first and second coming of Christ, the present temporal world is governed by the imperfect structures of the state and its coercive power. This City of Man is not ruled by the Gospel but rather by the principle of self-love. For Augustine, the earthly city was symbolic of the fallen state of man and could not adequately incorporate perfect justice or mercy toward its citizens. A Christian state would, however, have a closer relationship to the idealized City of God insofar as it realized the Christian ideals in its governmental principles and actions.

The "two cities" approach to the Christian philosophy of history would dominate the political theology of Europe for the next ten centuries, and allowed for the growth of a more secular understanding of temporal society. The Church was recognized as the only "perfect society," and the state was considered a kind of "necessary evil" that would exist until the end of human history at the Last Judgment. Augustine removed the aura of divine authority from the agency of the state and laid the foundation for a fully secularized civic order that would gradually take hold in Europe over many centuries. The Church retained a tenuous hold over European society for the next millennium, but the seeds of rebellion against her authority were planted long before the sixteenth century, when Martin Luther posted his ninety-five theses on the Church door at Wittenberg. The growth of autonomous centers of authority in Western culture were part of the reason that the Scientific Revolution occurred in Europe in the seventeenth century but did not occur, for example, in other areas of the world, where somewhat autonomous institutions such as the university and city states did not evolve as they did in the West.

Augustine's theory of knowledge was based, in part, on his Platonic understanding of "grades" of knowledge. The lowest level of understanding occurs with sensation and sensible objects. The highest level of knowledge pertains to the contemplation of eternal objects such as the divine beauty. Between these two levels of sense knowledge and incorporeal knowledge, Augustine posited a middle level which was characterized by the use of reason to bring about desired ends through our actions. Reason, used to clarify eternal matters such as in theology, was considered of a higher order because it led to contemplation, rather than to any particular action. Augustine presumed that contemplation was not a disinterested appreciation of the truth or beauty (as found in Plato), but rather the search by all human beings for ultimate happiness and beatitude in the vision of the God as revealed through Christ. Plato's "God" was ultimately impersonal, whereas Augustine's was personal and trinitarian in nature. Augustine did not accept the emanation theory of Plotinus but he did hold that the eternal Idea existed in the mind of God. These Ideas were the exemplars for all created reality.

Augustine's theory of illumination was similar to that of Plotinus but contained essential differences. For Plotinus, the One or God is the same as the light of the sun. The power of the sun radiates its essence into the material objects of the world through subordinate intelligible ideas. Augustine, however, held that that there was a kind of incorporeal light which fulfilled the same function for the soul as corporeal light did for the human eye. Just as the sunlight makes material objects visible to the human eye, so does the incorporeal spiritual light illumine the soul to "see" eternal truths. The human mind cannot "ascend" to the level of eternal truths without some assistance from the divine being. For Augustine, this assistance was necessary because no rational human being could apprehend eternal and unchanging truths with a rational mind that was temporal and transitory in its basic nature. This doctrine of divine illumination as found in Augustine would inspire Grossteste and Bacon in the thirteenth century. However, they added other elements to this theory which gave a unique place to mathematical reasoning within the Augustinian theory of illumination.

In the early fifth century, when Augustine wrote the *City of God*, a kind of philosophical and spiritual dualism had taken hold in the West. The imminent coming of the Kingdom of God proclaimed in the New Testament was replaced by the sacramental mediating functions of the Church. The "world" was viewed as the domain of the ungodly "earthly" city of man. The goal of life was to reach the spiritual "godly" city of the New Jerusalem located in heaven, fully realized only after death. Man's positive role in the process of salvation was diminished based upon the Augustinian doctrines of grace and predestination. The earlier idea of the Cosmic Christ, who is the Second Adam within a new created order, is replaced by the Christ of the Last Judgment who "separates the sheep from the goats" at the Last Judgment.

Augustine believed that, due to man's "fallen" nature, humanity was incapable of reaching God without divine intervention. "Fallen" nature was seen as a heavy weight that had to be overcome through ascetical practices. Sexual desire was considered the after-effect of Original Sin (*fomes peccati*) and marriage was considered a lower form of the Christian life. Only through the celibate or virginal life could the soul be elevated beyond the grip of the "earthly" downward pull of gravity. The Neoplatonic dimension of Augustine's thought emphasized the transitory nature of the temporal and the permanence of man's true home in the realm of the heavenly city. According to Richard Tarnas

> Augustine was the most modern of the ancients: he possessed an existentialist's self-awareness with his highly developed capacity for self-introspection, his concern with memory and consciousness and time, his psychological perspicacity, his doubt and remorse, his sense of the solitary alienation of the human self without God, his intensity of inner conflict, his intellectual skepticism and sophistication."[13]

Augustine was confronted with a crumbling Roman empire in the face of barbarian invasions, and he did not see many signs of human progress. The "world" was tainted by original sin and man's proclivity to concupiscence and greed. The only hope for mankind was outside the realm of human history in the spiritual realm as proclaimed by the Church in its sacramental life. Augustine retained some elements of his earlier Manichean spirituality which presumed a kind of eternal battle between good and evil. Human flesh was considered to be under the domain of original sin, and only the spiritual soul redeemed through grace could enter man's true home in the heavenly realm.

The split between the secular world of Nature and the spiritual world of the Church was confirmed within the Augustinian perspective of the City of Man and the City of God. The Augustinian view of Nature was vastly different from that of the Greek Fathers of the Patristic period, according to Jaroslav Pelikan and Matthew Fox. According to Pelikan, the Greek Fathers of the fourth and fifth century were more attuned to the Cosmic Christ because they had a different understanding of the "fall" of Adam and Eve. In the Greek view, sin is a relapse into a kind of "non-being." The "fall, both of humanity and of the world, was a loss of the tenuous hold on true being and therefore a fall into the abyss ... this view of the human condition did concentrate on death as corruptibility and transiency rather than on death as guilt and the 'wages of sin.' (Rom 6:23)."[14] Matthew Fox, commenting on this divergence between the Greek Fathers and Augustine, states that Augustine's

> ...interest was not in the cosmos but in psychological introspection and the question of personal guilt and salvation. He (Augustine), more than other Western figure, influenced the Christian West to be individualistic. The individualism of Descartes, who in the seventeenth century would declare "I think, therefore, I am," is immediately traceable to Augustine.[15]

---

[1] Matthew Fox, *The Coming of the Cosmic Christ* (San Francisco: Harper and Row, 1988), 88.

[2] Ibid., 83.

[3] Elaine Pagels, *Beyond Belief: The Secret Gospel of Thomas* (NY: Random House, 2003).

[4] Ibid., 86.

[5] Ralph P. Martin and Peter H. Davids, eds., *Dictionary of the Later New Testament and its Development* (Downers Grove, IL: InterVarsity Press, 1997), 707.

[6] For a detailed discussion of Ptolemy and his influence on ancient astronomy and astrology, see John North, *The Fontana History of Astronomy and Cosmology* (London: Fontana, 1994), 104 – 124.

[7] Quoted in Elaine Pagels, *The Gnostic Gospels* (NY: Vintage, 1981), xvi.

[8] Ibid., 159 – 160.

[9] For more detailed information on Clement of Alexandria and Origen, see F.L. Cross, ed., *The Oxford Dictionary of the Christian Church* (London: Oxford University Press, 1958).

[10] For the history of biblical scholarship see Christopher De Hamel, *The Book: A History of the Bible* (London: Phaidon Press, 2001). See also the first translation of the Gospels into English in Michelle P. Brown's scholarly study *The Lindisfarne Gospels: Society, Spirituality and the Scribe* (London: The British Library, 2003.)

[11] A contemporary presentation of the philosophy and spirituality of time can be found in Eckhart Tolle's *The Power of Now* (Novato, CA: New World Library, 1990).

[12] Stephen Hawkings, *A Brief History of Time*, 10th edition (NY: Bantam Doubleday, 1998).

[13] Richard Tarnas, *The Passion of the Western Mind* (NY: Ballantine, 1993), 143 – 144.

[14] Jaroslav Pelikan, *Jesus Through the Centuries* (New York: Harper and Row, 1985), 68.

[15] Matthew Fox, *The Coming of the Cosmic Christ* (San Francisco: Harper and Row, 1986), 108.

Discussion Questions

1) What was the Gnostic understanding of the material universe?

2) How did Irenaeus attempt to thwart the influence of the Gnostic theology?

3) What role did philosophy play in Christian theology during the Patristic era?

4) How did the Canon of Scripture play a role in defining the nature of faith for Christians?

5) What philosophical principles were important in the dialogue between faith and reason in the Patristic era?

6) What were the philosophical principles that informed the thought of St. Augustine?

7) How did Augustine's understanding of history (the Two Cities) affect future interpretations of faith and reason?

Chapter Six

Islam and Science

Islamic astronomers were open to the contributions that they found in other cultures. As we shall see in the field of medicine, Islamic scholars interacted with and drew extensively **from Jewish and Christian medical philosophers and scientists.**

The earliest attempt at a classification of scientific thought within Islam occurred with the Arab philosopher and scientist, Al-Farabi (870 – 950 CE). He was often called the "Second Master" (after Aristotle) because of his facility in both philosophy and the natural sciences. He is also known as the "Father of Islamic Neoplatonism." In the Latin West, he was known as Abunaser. Much of his writing was influenced by Neoplatonic theories of emanation. He did, however, recognize the value of knowledge discovered through music, philosophy and the Aristotelian natural sciences. Like Plato, Al-Farabi wrote an important work on political philosophy entitled *The Virtuous City*. In his *Book of the Enumeration of the Sciences*, (*Kitab ihsa' al-'ulum*), Al-Farabi developed the first Islamic interpretation of the full range of knowledge available to humanity within a Neoplatonic and Islamic perspective.

Within the Neoplatonic view of metaphysics, the deity does not have direct contact with the earthly realm; instead, it acts through a series of intermediary steps or intelligences that emanate from the ultimate source. These steps lead down to the origin of the human intellect, which has several dimensions. For Al-Farabi, all knowledge had its source in the First Intellect, which emanated from the deity or First Existence or the One.

In the *Book of the Enumeration of the Sciences,* Al-Farabi divided all knowledge into five chapters or sections. The first chapter dealt with the knowledge of language and corresponds to the study of rhetoric or public speaking in the West. The second chapter also deals with language but from the perspective of proper modes of demonstration, such as we find in Aristotelian Logic. The third chapter was devoted to the mathematical sciences, including astronomy and astrology, while the fourth chapter dealt with physics and metaphysics. The fifth chapter focused on the social sciences such as jurisprudence, political science and scholastic theology or sacred law. Al-Farabi accepted the Ptolemaic understanding of the heavens as composed of concentric spheres; the "highest" sphere originated motion and passed it on to the other spheres, the lowest of which was the lunar sphere. Ten intelligences produced the "souls" for each of the celestial spheres. The tenth intelligence presided over the sublunary world, and acted as the source for all physical forms and prime matter. Because of the importance of the celestial realm in Islamic Neoplatonism and in the interpretation of Qu'ranic passages, the study of astronomy became an important part of the Islamic sciences. Ptolemy remained the central figure in the Islamic conceptualization of the heavens, although the tables used to compute the movements of stars were largely drawn from Persian and Indian sources. Islamic astronomers were open to the contributions that they found in other cultures. As we shall see in the field of medicine, Islamic scholars interacted with and drew extensively from Jewish and Christian medical philosophers and scientists.

Astronomy

Muslim contributions in astronomy provided a link between the ancient Greek world and modern astronomy. Western astronomy began to incorporate Islamic knowledge of the heavens in the tenth and eleventh centuries, mainly via contact with Islamic science in Spain. Gerbert of Aurillac (c. 945 – 1003) returned to continental Europe from northern Spain with astronomical treatises that were previously unknown in Europe. Through this contact with the Spanish Islamic culture, treatises on the astrolabe were translated from Arabic into Latin. The incorporation of the astrolabe into Western culture helped orient astronomy toward a mathematical understanding of the planets and the stars. Adelard of Bath made a significant contribution to this movement when he translated the astronomical tables of Al-Khwarazmi (d. after 847) from Arabic into Latin in 1126. Al-Khwarazmi was one of the most notable mathematicians of the ancient and medieval world. The mathematical science of algebra and the word "algorithm" are forever linked to his name, *al-jabr*, in Arabic. Other astronomical tables were translated in Toledo soon afterward, placing astronomy on a sounder, scientific basis. Nevertheless, in Islamic astronomy, the science of the heavens always had a spiritual dimension, and was viewed as a revelation of the divine unity expressed in mathematical laws governing the movement of the heavenly bodies. Ptolemy had constructed mathematical laws to make sense of the planetary phenomena, but Islamic astronomers constructed a physical model of the universe which Ptolemy never had.

The tendency toward the "physical" interpretation of the heavens was already evident in the writings of the ninth century astronomer and mathematician, Thabit ibn Qurra (826 – 901 CE), especially in his treatise on the constitution of the heavens. Although the original of this treatise seems to have been lost, excerpts in the works of many later writers, including Maimonides and Albertus Magnus, indicate that Thabit ibn Qurra had conceived of the heavens as solid spheres with a compressible fluid between the orbs and eccentrics. [1]

The most famous astronomical treatise from the ancient world, Ptolemy's *Almagest*, was translated from the Arabic by Gerard of Cremona, working in Toledo during the latter half of the twelfth century. Ptolemy's catalogue of the stars included a scale of magnitude from the brightest to the least visible of the stars. Almost every Muslim astronomer in the medieval world had a *zij*, an astronomical table that was used to record observations and calculations about the planets and starts. The astrolabe was their rudimentary "computer" to determine the altitude and azimuth of celestial bodies. Although the astrolabe can be traced back to the Greek astronomer, Hipparchus, Muslims added the alidade, which was a kind of pointer or sighting device, which enabled the astronomer to determine the altitude of a star or planet.

Almost all ancient civilizations held the view that the earth, the abode of man, was at rest at the center of the universe and that the heavenly bodies revolved around it. The Egyptians believed that the sky was the arched body of a goddess; the Babylonians thought that it was shaped like a bell jar, and the Indians believed that the world rested on the tusks of a huge elephant. The Chinese considered the earth as an upturned bowl and the sky, another concentric bowl covered the earth bowl. In Greece, it was said that the number of cosmologists was equal to that of philosophers, and there were quite a large number of them. Several of them believed in a geocentric universe, that is, that all heavenly bodies moved around the earth. Anaximander believed that there were many other worlds like ours. Aristarchus, on the other hand, propounded that the earth and the planets revolved round the sun. But for about two thousand years, belief about the universe was dominated by the physics of Aristotle. He taught that the spherical earth was at the center of the universe and that the universe was perfectly ordered, with the regions above the moon (the superlunary region), divine, indestructible and incorruptible; and the region below the moon (the sublunary region), destructible and corruptible.

Comets brought suspicion to this theory. Comets had to be recognized as destructible, but observation showed that they were superlunary, therefore, these objects invading the earth had to be accepted as destructible. Thus arose suspicion about Aristotle's theory.

Aristotle had taught that superlunary bodies were divine. They were perfect and their motions were perfect. A circle, according to him, was the perfect figure; and circular motion was regarded as the perfect motion. All motions of superlunary bodies, he stated, should be interpreted in terms of circular motion. As man is the supreme creation and as the earth is the abode of man, all circular motions should have earth as the center. Aristotle's theory did not, however, explain the motions of the planets against the background of fixed stars, since the movement of the planets across the sky appeared to be irregular.

Astronomy at that time was concerned only with the "saving of the phenomenon," that is, interpreting the apparent motions of the planets with the help of circular orbits with the earth at the center. Ptolemy, in the second century, completed the interpretation of the orbits of the planets with the help of circular motions. To demonstrate the irregular motion of a planet as made up of circular motions, it was said that the planets actually moved on circles, whose center moved on another circle, whose center was the earth. The first circle, on which the planet moved, was called the epicycle; the second circle on which the center of the epicycle moved was called the deferent. One epicycle and one deferent, however, were not enough to explain the motions of all the planets. As many as thirty-nine epicycles and deferents were necessary to explain the motions of all the planets.

Ptolemy was the authority. His method was used to "save the phenomenon" with a network of epicycles and deferents, by demonstrating that all the phenomenon of the sky could be explained or saved with the help of uniform circular motions. Astronomers in India followed this method; there the epicycle was called _Shighra Britta_ and the deferent was called _Manda Britta_. In

Arabic, these are *Tadbir* and *Montaqa* respectively. These metaphysical ideas, together with the earth-centered universe and Aristotle's idea about circular motions, were first doubted by the Muslim astronomer

Al-Zarqali in the eleventh century.

> To the latter half of this century (eleventh century CE) belongs the first outstanding Spanish observational astronomer, al Zarqali. He invented a new astronomical instrument called *sahifah* (*Saphaea ar-zachelis*), which became widely known; he is also credited with the explicit proof of the motion of the apogee of the sun with respect to the fixed stars. His most important contribution, however, is the editing of *Toledan Zij*, composed with the aid of several other Muslim and Jewish scientists and widely used by both the Latin and Muslim astronomers of later centuries. Spanish astronomy after Al-Zarqali developed in an anti-Ptolemaic vein, in the sense that criticism began to be made of the epicyclic theory. [2]

In the sixteenth century, ideas about the epicycles were challenged by Copernicus, and were completely discarded by Kepler and Newton in the seventeenth century. Newton removed the barrier between superlunary and sublunary bodies and brought the heavens and earth under the same laws of physics. It was so momentous a work that the poet Alexander Pope wrote: "When Nature and nature's laws lay hid by night, God said let Newton be and all was light," and these words became Newton's epitaph. However, the work was not Newton's alone. He said, "If I have seen farther than others, it is because I stood on the shoulders of giants." These giants included Thabit ibn Qurra, Copernicus, Kepler and Descartes.[3]

Muslim astronomers doubted the veracity of circular motions, but they hesitated to say that Ptolemy was wrong. All the Muslim astronomers made large numbers of observations and made tables out of them. Copernicus himself made only twenty-seven observations. However, he made elaborate use of the tables of observations by the Muslim astronomers, particularly the table of Thabit ibn Qurra which was accepted by later historians as accurate.[4] Thus the Muslim astronomers helped to establish a link between ancient astronomy and modern astronomy.

During the Middle Ages, Ptolemy's Greek book, the *Megale Syntaxis (the Great Treatise)* was considered to be an authority on astronomy. In the ninth century, Ibn-Ishaq translated this book into Arabic. While translating, the article *al* was added as a mark of respect and, considering the size of the volume, the superlative degree *megaste* was used instead of *megale*. Thus the book was named *Al-Megaste*, which ultimately took the form *Al-Magest*. It was believed that whatever was contrary to *Al-Magest* must be wrong. As has already been mentioned, some Muslim astronomers doubted the circular motion of the planets. However, since this contravened *Al-Magest*, it was not accepted and no further study of this topic was made. In the eleventh century, Al-Zarqali[5] (1028 – 1087 CE) even suggested that the planetary orbits were not circular, but elliptic. This was six hundred years before Kepler discovered his planetary laws. Again,

Al-Zarqali's idea was not accepted based on the uncritical acceptance of the *Al-Magest*. Thus, although the door of modern astronomy was open to the Muslim astronomers, they could not pass through it because of the unquestioned authority of *Al-Magest*. Ptolemy's *Al-Magest* reigned supreme in the field of astronomy for 1500 years. As Muslims began to show interest in astronomy, they began to translate books on the subject from Syriac and Greek into Arabic. Since the original books were not available, these books translated by the Muslims were retranslated from Arabic into Latin, French, English and other languages. This is evident from the fact that the names of a large number of stars are of Arabic origin. Sometimes it is difficult to reconstruct the original names in Arabic. In some cases, this is due to differences in pronunciation. Some of the main contributions of the Muslims in astronomy are the large number of *zijs*, that is, tables of observational data. Almost each of the Muslim astronomers had a *zij* of his own, made by his own observation. The Muslims paid importance to observation. Before the Muslim period, abstract arguments were preferred to observation. Ptolemy does not seem to have made many observations except of a few eclipses. His star catalogue is simply the reproduction of that of Hipparcus. This is evident from the fact that Ptolemy's catalogue does not contain those stars which were visible from Alexandria (place of work of Ptolemy). Also, they were not included in the catalogue by Hipparcus, since those stars were not visible from Rhodes (where Hipparcus worked). Muslim astronomers made diligent observations; they constructed new instruments and displayed more practical activity than the Greeks. In addition, the accuracy of their work often surpassed the results of antiquity. In the beginning, their aim, it seems, was to continue and verify the works of their predecessors, the Greeks.

More than 150 *zijs* are attributed to Muslim astronomers. Copernicus himself consulted these *zijs*, and considered the *zij* of Thabit ibn Qurra to be the most authoritative. With the help of these astronomical tables, Copernicus propounded his heliocentric theory, that is, a sun-centric universe. Though Copernicus said that the earth and the planets revolved around the sun, he held that they revolved in circular orbits. The difficulty of reconciling the irregular motion of the planets with circular motion remained. So he also had to utilize epicycles and deferents to explain his theory. The matter then became even more complicated, since more epicycles and deferents were necessary in Copernicus' system than in the system of Ptolemy.

In the sixteenth century, Tycho Brahe made extensive observations of the heavenly bodies.[6] It is from Brahe's list of observations that Kepler ultimately established the three basic laws of modern astronomy. Brahe himself believed in a geocentric solar system, but his disciple Kepler believed in the heliocentric system. As a result, Brahe did not allow Kepler to see all the data of his planetary observations; Kepler was able to use this data only after his teacher's death. Kepler worked very hard on this data to resolve discrepancies. He discovered that the circular orbit of Mars had an error of eight minutes of arc and his instruments were accurate to within one minute. He then realized that an elliptical orbit for Mars would conform exactly to Brahe's date. This discovery is now known as Kepler's First Law. He did not consider this as an error in observation as the Muslims did. Earlier, a Muslim scientist, Al-Battani (858 – 929 CE), determined the celestial longitude of the sun's perigee; his result differed from that of Ptolemy. Al-Battani believed that he himself was wrong, since it was assumed that Ptolemy could not be wrong. On the other hand, Kepler did not consider Brahe's observations to be infallible. He tried hard to get these 8' (eight minutes) of arc fitted into the orbit he determined. Ultimately, Kepler successfully discovered his first planetary law based upon Brahe's data. Brahe was certainly the master of observation, but he did mention that he had used the tables of observation by Abu'l Wafa (940 – 998 CE). Abu'l Wafa pointed out many errors in Ptolemy's calculations, but these were not seen as accurate at the time.

It has already been mentioned that all the Muslim astronomers made numerous observations of the heavens and compiled *zijs*. These tables, unfortunately, are no longer available. Modern astronomers do not even know which astronomer observed which heavenly bodies. Since Copernicus used the table of Thabit ibn-Qurra, it may be assumed that these tables contained observational data about the planets. Al-Khawarizmi, Ibn-Yunus, Abdur Rahman Sufi, Ulugh Begh and many others made observations about the stars.

In the second century BCE, Hipparcus prepared the first star catalogue. He tabulated 1000 stars and introduced a brightness classification. A later star catalogue by Ptolemy, created in the second century CE, was a simple reproduction of Hipparcus' catalogue, containing positions and magnitude (of brightness) of the stars. It was then that Muslim astronomers compiled additional star catalogues. Ulugh Begh's star catalogue was the only such catalogue; it was in use until Johannes Bayer (1564 – 1617) constructed his catalogue in the seventeenth century.

In fact, Ulugh Begh (1394 – 1499 CE) was one of the outstanding Muslim astronomers of the fifteenth century, and died just twenty years before the birth of Copernicus. He was the ruler of Samarkand (where his father built an observatory), and, along with fellow astronomers, he observed the motions and positions of stars and planets. As a result, he prepared a star catalogue, which was known as *Zij-i-Ulugh Begh*. It was also called *zij-I-Sultani*. Ulugh Begh's *zij* was unique in that he, for the first time, denoted the positions of the stars in terms of celestial latitude and longitude. The *zij* had a list of 1018 stars, which became a standard star catalogue until Tycho Brahe's time. Of the 1018 stars mentioned in the *zij-I-Sultani*, Ulugh Begh observed all but seventeen stars of the Southern Constellations. For these stars, he added a constant number to the longitudes determined by Ptolemy. He followed Nasir al-Din al-Tusi's *Zij-Ilkhani* as the basis for his observations. He established a *madrasa* in Samarkand that became one of the most notable research centers for science and mathematics in the fifteenth century.

Ulug Begh's also explored new frontiers in trigonometry and physical geometry. The Arab/Muslim world should be credited with the invention of both algebra and trigonometry. Arab mathematicians also introduced Arabic numerals into Europe to replace the archaic Roman numerals.

There are many aspects of astronomy that were investigated by the Muslim astronomers. Al-Biruni (973 – 1048 CE), in his *Qunun-i-Masud*, mentioned two motions of the earth. He also stated that one of these motions was the motion of rotation about the axis. As the earth rotates about its axis, with the earth appearing to circulate in both directions, it seems to intersect the celestial sphere in two points called the poles. The plane, passing through the center of the earth and perpendicular to the axis of rotation, seems to intersect the earth in a great circle called the terrestrial equator, and the celestial sphere in a great circle, known as the celestial equator. Again, the orbit in which the sun appears to move among the fixed stars in the course of a year is another great circle; the ecliptic and the celestial equator intersect one another at points called equinoctial points. The axis of rotation of the earth, however, is not fixed. It "wobbles" and makes a complete revolution in 26,000 years. As the axis wobbles, the equatorial plane perpendicular to it also shifts position. Since such points of intersection of the celestial equator with the elliptic also shift position, this shifting of position of the equinoctial points is known as precession of equinoxes. It is now known that the rate of precession of equinoxes is 50.2 seconds per year. Almost all Muslim astronomers investigated the angle of inclination and the rate of precession. Antonie Pannekoeck maintains that the importance of Arabian astronomy lay in fact that it preserved the science of antiquity in translations, commentaries, interpretations and new observations, and handed it down to the Christian world. Thus it considerably influenced the initial development of scientific astronomy in medieval Europe.[7]

Muslims of the Middle Ages had several reasons to pursue astronomy. First, since the Muslim culture was the successor to the ancient Babylonian civilization, the Muslims had inherited a passion for the subject. Second, the Muslims felt obliged to accurately determine the positions of heavenly bodies so that (when Muslims resided in foreign lands) they could ascertain the exact location of the *Qibla* and correctly determine the times for daily prayers. However, the greatest impetus to the study of astronomy came from the translation of two astronomical works, one Indian and the other Greek. The first treatise was translated by the great astronomer Abu Abdullah Solaiman ibn Ibrahim al-Farazi, or simply Farazi II. He lived during the time of Khalifah al-Mamun (813 – 833 CE). Another astronomer of this period, Yakub ibn Tariq, worked with Farazi II in the translation of *Sind Hind*. Farazi II was the first to prepare a table of sines with half-degree differences.

The second famous book on astronomy was the *Syntaxis* by the Greek astronomer Ptolemy. This work was translated by the astronomers in the court of Khalifah al-Mamun and was called *Al-Magest* in Arabic. It is important to note that Ishaq ibn Hunain was among the translators of this work.[8]

Astronomy and Astrophysics in the Qu'ran

In some of the verses of the Qu'ran, we find references to celestial bodies like the sun, the moon, stars, heavens and the earth. Regarding the sun and the moon, God made the sun as a glorious lamp and the moon a light in the midst of seven heavens (Qu'ran, 71: 15, 16). They are subject to God's laws (Qu'ran, 7: 54; 13: 2; 31: 29) and command (Qu'ran, 16: 12). They swim along each in its rounded courses (Qu'ran, 21:33) following courses exactly computed (Qu'ran, 55: 5), each in its own orbit. Each runs its course for an appointed term (Qu'ran, 31: 29). In this course of movement, the sun cannot catch up to the moon (Qu'ran, 36: 38, 39). Celestial bodies are used for reckoning time (Qu'ran, 6: 96, 97). One day the sun will be folded up and the moon will be cleft asunder (Qu'ran, 54: 1). Regarding the stars, it has been stated that they are as beacons to guide through the dark spaces of land and sea (Qu'ran, 6: 96, 97) but they are also governed by God's laws and are under His command (Qu'ran, 7: 54). Stars exist in the lower heaven for beauty and they work as guards against all obstinate rebellious evil spirits (Qu'ran, 37: 9, 10). One day stars would become dim (Qu'ran, 77: 9, 8) and fall, loosing their luster, and would be scattered (Qu'ran, 82: 1, 2). One of the stars referred to in the Qu'ran is Sirius (Qu'ran, 53, 49), described as a mighty star. A star of piercing brightness is also referred to in the verse (Qu'ran, 86: 1, 3). We have some idea about the sun, the moon, the stars and the earth, which we see every day, but this cannot be said about the heavens and the signs of the zodiac. The natural question that may arise here: what are they, and where are they? They are not in the category of the sun, the moon and the stars that we see directly around us. Though we know only one earth, we have no direct idea of the seven earths referred to the Qu'ran. Is this earth of ours one of the seven? If so, where are the others? Therefore, for the heavens, earth and zodiac signs, men must speculate, which is not necessary for the sun, the moon and the stars. To begin to understand this difficult creation of God let us try to analyze the matters of these celestial bodies one by one.

Ptolemaic astronomy explains the motion of the heavenly bodies. Ptolemy systemized the ideas of the ancient people regarding the seven moving heavenly bodies, which he called "planets." He observed that the seven heavenly bodies do move about from one place to another, each with a particular course. He thought that these seven bodies must have their own will or influence. These seven bodies are (1) the sun; (2) the moon (which, it was found, influences the tides, the temperature and life on earth); (3) Mercury; and (4) Venus (which appear as morning and evening stars); (5) Mars, (6) Jupiter, and (7) Saturn. Ptolemy's theory was that the earth is stationary, at the center of the universe, and that these planets revolve around it. This doctrine of Ptolemy, known as the geo-centric system, was accepted as truth by the ancient astronomers and remained as such up to the sixteenth century. This system, however, does not properly account for the seven heavens, the seven earths and the seven tracts of the Qu'ran. Various ingenious suggestions have been put forward to reconcile the Qu'ranic version with this theory. According to one idea, it is held that since the word *sama* (heaven) refers to what we see above us, and that every heaven is a heaven in relation to what is beneath it and an earth in relation to what is above it. Another idea is that the seven earths referred to the Qu'ran may be the seven major planets of the solar system.

Next we consider the matter of stars. The Qu'ran refers to stars in various places. As mentioned earlier, they decorate the lower heavens and guard against obstinate rebellious evil spirits, but they are governed by laws, as well. The Qu'ran, however, does not speak about the number of stars in the sky and does not mention specifics about any star except Sirius. It is the brightest fixed star in the sky and attracted the attention of the ancient people. The pagan Arabs worshipped it as a divinity. It is perhaps this star that has been referred to in verse 76 of *Surah Anam* in connection with the Prophet Abraham, "He saw a star and said this is my Lord" (Qu'ran, 6: 76). The star of piercing brightness which is called *Tariq* and is referred to in the Qu'ran, is understood by some Muslim scholars to be the morning star, by some the planet Saturn, by some

Sirius, by others, shooting stars. In the Qu'ran God speaks of decorating the heavens with stars. How many stars are there? What are the laws, which govern these stars? Today, we know that the number of stars seen by the naked eye on the clearest night is about 6000. The invention of the telescope and the improved quality of astronomical observations have made great changes in astronomers' ideas about the number of stars. Astronomers now surmise that the number of stars may be as many as forty billion.

Some scholars think that the Muslims were inspired by the Qu'ran to study scientific subjects. They pointed out that we must not be surprised to find that the Qu'ran was regarded as the fountainhead of all the sciences. Every subject connected with heaven or earth, human life, commerce and various trades is occasionally touched upon in the Qu'ran, and this gave rise to the production of commentaries on parts of the holy book. In this way, the Qu'ran was responsible for learned discussions, and it indirectly influenced the development of many branches of science in the Muslim world. This not only affected the Arabs but it inspired Jewish philosophers to treat metaphysical and religious questions according to Islamic methods. Within Islam, spiritual activity was not confined to theological speculations alone. Acquaintance with the philosophical, astronomical and medical writings of the Greeks led to the pursuit of these studies. In his descriptive revelations, Mohammad repeatedly calls attention to the movements of the heavenly bodies. He indicates they are parts of the miracles of Allah, created to serve man, and not to be worshipped. How successfully Muslim scholars pursued the study of astronomy is shown by the fact that for centuries they were its principal supporters. Even now, many Arabic star names and technical terms are in use. In interpreting the verse

> And the sun runs his course for a period determined for him: that is the decree of (Him), the exalted in mighty, the all-knowing. And the moon—we have measured for her mansions to traverse till she returns like the old (and withered) lower part of a date-stalk. It is not permitted

for the sun to catch up the moon, nor can the night outstrip the day; each (just) swims along in (its own) orbit (according to law)" (Qu'ran, _Surah Yasin_: 38, 39, 40).

some scholars point out that Mohammad wished to express the idea that the movements of the sun and the moon were so well-regulated that it is the latter which reaches the former and not vice-versa. On the occasion of a total solar eclipse, Mohammad said that it did not cause the death of any man, yet he recited special prayers during the eclipse. Traditionally, he has always been seen as a great astronomer. Muslim astronomers, like many ancient and medieval astronomers, had an unflinching belief in ancient knowledge and respect for sages like Ptolemy and Aristotle. If the Muslim astronomers had properly analyzed the facts collected by them with care and self-confidence, they would have probably realized the defect in Ptolemy's geocentric system long before Copernicus and Galileo. Along with the stars we may consider the matters of the sun and the moon. They are moving in their orbits following courses exactly computed (Qu'ran 55: 5). Anyone reading this description should be mindful of it while investigating the orbit of the sun and moon and the laws to which they are subject. This requires scholars to study the movement of the sun and the moon most minutely and scientifically to find out the laws they are following in their movements. This can be done only through the science of astronomy.

According to the Qu'ran, God has whispered about the zodiac signs/mansions of the moon in these verses. This is all the more significant since the Greeks had no lunar mansion in their astronomy. It will depend upon future scholars to investigate the zodiac signs/mansion of the moon.

Although Muslim astronomers have scientifically investigated the matter, modern commentators have turned their eyes to this aspect of the Qu'ran from a spiritual point of view. It is said that the zodiac marks the sun's path through the heavens year after year and limits of the wanderings of the moon and the planets. We make twelve divisions of it and call them signs of the zodiac. Each marks the solar path through the heavens as we see it, month after month. We can thus mark off the seasons in our solar year and express in specific laws the most important facts in meteorology, agriculture and the seasonal winds and tides. Then there are the mansions of the moon, the mapping out of the constellations and the other elegant facts of the heaven, some of which affect our physical life on this earth. Even after saying all these, some turn towards spiritual interpretations and, truly, the highest lessons we can derive from these writings are spiritual. The result of this kind of spiritual interpretation has been that the whole significance of God's message calls us toward practical investigations of the natural world.

The following verse alludes to the achievement of Babylon in different branches of science, especially in astronomy.

> But the evil ones, teaching men magic, and such things as came down at Babylon to the angels Harut and Marut. But neither of these taught any one (such things) without saying "We are only for trial; so do not blaspheme" (Qu'ran 2: 102).

Marut is no doubt an Arabic version of Marduk, a defied king of Babylon worshipped as a god of astrology/magic in Babylon. In ancient times, astronomy was synonymous with astrology, a pseudo-science used to predict the course of human destinies by signs derived from the positions of the heavenly bodies. As a matter of fact, astronomy was initially pursued more for astrological purposes than for pure astronomical purposes and observations. This was certainly the case in Babylon. Inscriptions on Assyrian tablets show that astronomy was used for astrological purposes.

According to some, Harut and Marut were kings and are referred to as such in the Qu'ran. The names Harut and Marut curiously resemble the names of two archangels, Hauravatat and Amertat, which mean health, fertility and immortality.

According to the Qu'ran, Harut and Marut taught science with the admonition that it should not be used for evil purposes. Though astrology is condemned in these verses, astrologers were greatly honored at the courts of the Caliphs, emperors and kings. Muslim astrologers made use of the twelve signs of the zodiac and represented their work as science. They assumed that (1) human life depends upon phenomena in nature, for instance, the fertility of the soil is due to sunshine and rain, and (2) moonlight and sunshine cause happiness and misery to things on earth. When the effect of moonlight and sunshine on plants, animals and human beings is visible, the same holds with other planets, as well, though to a lesser extent.

Theologians opposed astrology because they suspected that the action of the stars on human destiny were a menace to the power and will to God. Strict Islamic monotheism could not tolerate the idea of spheres possessing souls and their movements determining the happiness or the misery of human beings on earth. Jewish and Christian theologians came to the same conclusion about the influence of the heavens on human destiny. All three monotheistic religions recognized the influence of the heavens upon earthly matters but did not want this influence to infringe upon God's providential presence, human freedom or a person's spiritual condition. Interest in the heavenly realms among all three monotheistic religions indicates that they were seeking a cosmic spirituality rather than just personal salvation for their adherents.

Chemistry

The importance of acquiring "knowledge" in Islam dates back to the first revelation of the Qu'ran; in a broad sense it emphasized the learning of all sciences including the attributes of the Creator of human life and of the material universe. The entire material structures of the universe have been considered as the manifestation of the creation of a Supreme Being and it is for man to understand and to derive benefit from these creations. Man and his whole environment are composed of elements and their compounds, which have been assembled in various ways through processes according to certain definite laws. Thus, many physical phenomena observed daily by people draw the attention of men of knowledge to the study of the elements and the structures of various substances. There are about fifty verses in the Qu'ran relating to the material world, which actually embody the subject matter of the science of chemistry. Thus inspired by the teachings of the Qu'ran and the instructions received from men of knowledge, the contributions to chemical sciences laid down the foundation for the development of chemistry to a point from where it could easily continue into modern times for applications and usage.

The foundation and the infrastructures of the knowledge of chemistry were extended, enlarged and broadened to make chemistry a distinct discipline of human learning for the welfare of mankind. In addition, chemistry would play an important role in the historical changes resulting in the rise and fall of nations and civilizations. According to Sarton, the foundation of modern chemistry was actually laid by Al-Razi, one of the celebrated personalities of science in the medieval period.[9]

Nishapur in Iran became the early seat of learning at a time when Islam was just spreading its areas of influence. Greek sciences were at the lowest ebb in the Byzantine Empire because of the persecution of the Nestorians. The Nestorians took refuge in Nishapur in order to escape Byzantine persecution. It is here that Muslim scholars and intellectuals first came in contact with the Nestorians, which ultimately resulted in the transfer of knowledge and development of sciences with renewed zeal. It is reported that with the rise of the Abbasid Caliphs, Baghdad rapidly replaced Nishapur and Damascus as the seat of power and learning. Simultaneously, on the far Western side of the European continent, a number of institutes were established in Spain under the patronage of a branch of Umayyad rulers. Khalid Bin Yazid started to acquire knowledge in chemistry from the Alexandrian writings that were the main sources of the scientific knowledge of the Greeks. Thousands of years before this, the Egyptians had developed a knowledge of chemistry and successfully applied this knowledge, particularly for mummification.

The Muslim enthusiasm for learning was intense. Schools and centers of learning were founded in many towns and cities. Observatories, laboratories and libraries were founded and it is on record that Hakim II of Spain (961 – 976) had in his library more than 600,000 volumes indexed in forty-four volumes. In contrast, the Royal Library in France (founded in the fifth century) consisted of only 900 volumes; many of these were Latin translations of Arabic books.

The Origin of the Word "Chemistry"

The Arabic word *Al-Kimya* appears to be the root of the modern English term "chemistry" or the German *chemie*. However, the introduction of the word into the Arabic language might have come from the old Egyptian word *khem* or *chem*, which means "black." This occurs in hieroglyphics and is used in Greek by Plutarch in the form of *chemia*. The practice of chemistry was termed the "Art of *Khem*" or "Black Art." Since humanity has long held the desire to create a substance that would bring everlasting life or turn base metals into gold, mystery is inherent in the practice of the "Art." The quest for eternal life needs no explanation. The transformation of base metals into gold would be of considerable economic important to any who could successfully perform such a feat.

The idea that the word *chim-eya* (possibly meaning plant juice for gold making) is of Chinese origin does not seem to be tenable, since there was no contact between the Arabs and the Chinese before the advent of Islam. It was only after the Islamic civilization spread to Eastern China that the Muslims appear to have developed large-scale contact and interaction with the Chinese.

Here it may be noted that the term "Arab" must be taken in a broad sense and must include all those who were politically under the Arab rule and used the Arab language. This did not necessarily include those who professed the religion of Islam or were Muslims of non-Arab origin. For example, Persian literature and religion diverged in their own directions, but moved into the spheres of influence of the starting-point of Arabic culture, and there was sufficient coherence in the entire community (under the rule of Khalifahs) from the very beginning of the Islamic expansion. People of all races used Arabic. It gradually replaced the languages of Greek, Syrian, and Persian as the language of culture, science and administration. Initially, the Arab civilization arose in the seventh century with little learned culture of its own. Within a few centuries, however, it had drawn upon Syrian and Greek culture, philosophy and science and had developed a unique culture of its own.

Gerard of Cremona was one of many prominent scholars who translated scientific and philosophical works from Arabic to Latin in the Middle Ages. His translations made decisive contributions to the growth of medieval Latin science. He is said to have translated some eighty-two books, including books on chemistry. Another scholar who brought the science of chemistry to Western Europe some 800 years ago was Robert of Chester (Robertus Anglicus). Following the custom of the time, Robert studied at the Moorish schools in Spain. The Moors were the world's leading scientists at that period. Robert is said to have completed the translation of an Arabic treatise on chemistry into Latin in 1144. This work is considered to be Europe's first chemical textbook. Robert is also reported to have made the first Latin translation of the Qu'ran, and he translated the celebrated book on algebra by Khwarizmi. In addition, he introduced the flowing Arab robes which are now the academic gowns of the universities all over the world.

Yet another notable personality in the early transfer of knowledge to Europe was Michael Scot, who flourished in the early thirteenth century. He is seen as a controversial figure (as is usually the case for legends surrounding such historical personalities) and he was active as a translator in Toledo, Spain. In 1217, he translated al-Bitruji's book *On the Sphere*, one known as *De al Chimia, On Medicine* and many others on various subjects. Although he made no important scientific discovery, his greatest single achievement was the opening up of the study of Aristotle in the West by his translation of the commentaries of Averroes and ibn-Haitham.

Albert Magnus (d. 1280) also translated a large number of books from Arabic to Latin, including the *Book of Talisman* and a book on alchemy written by al-Washiyah. Peter of Abano is also regarded as one of the most typical of the Arabists who lived toward the middle of the thirteenth century. From 1222, Padua was already a seat of a university. Peter traveled to various countries and was responsible for large number of translations of many science books, particularly those on medicine. In the medieval school of Padua, Avicenna held the same high place as Averroes in the philosophy of science. Robert of Chester also translated some books from Latin to English, which later on became some of the main sources of important records of the scientific achievements of his time.

A Muslim scientist, Khalid bin Yazid (d. 704) consulted many Greek sources on philosophy and science and translated many of the books into Arabic, particularly those on chemistry, astronomy and medicine. He may be regarded as a pioneer in this field. It is said that he learned chemistry from Morienus Romanus, a Greek scholar, and that he wrote a number of epistles including a book of poetry. Morienus himself appears to be a controversial figure. In 1144, Robert of Chester translated the Arabic *Book of Khalid* into Latin (*Liber De Composition Alchemiae.*)

In the tenth century, Al-Razi resolved the difference of opinion regarding the contributions of Khalid to the field of chemistry. In his book *Kitabul Asrar* (*Book of Secrets*)[10], Al-Razi wrote an introduction which names Khalid bin Yazid as one of the celebrated chemists of an earlier period. Because of the ravages of the time, many of the books written by Khalid appear to have been lost or could not be attributed to him. In *On the Noble Art and its Principles*, Khalid includes the procedures for the preparation of dyes and colors. The author used allegories in which the names of the planets represent material substances on earth which he used for the practice of alchemical art; this may be regarded as an early attempt to invent symbols for chemical substances. Khalid also made a reference to "Stephanus" from whom he learned the art of alchemy, particularly the method of gold making. His other contributions include "Preparation of Divine Water," "Gases from Stones," "Self –freezing of Water," "Making of the White Gold," "Dyeing and Coloring," "Combinations of Solids and Gases" and others. It is generally acknowledged that an accurate balance for weighing chemicals was in use during the time of Khalid. Another celebrated alchemist is Jabir ibn Hayyan. Although he has been associated with activities which appear to have more to do with the art of alchemy than with science, his contributions to the development of science during the Middle Ages and the early period of the Islamic civilization are seen as significant. According to ibn-Nadim's *Fihrist*, Jabir lived in Kufa during the time of Harun-ar-Rashid (Caliph from 786 to 809). Jabir was a physician, astronomer, mathematician, and chemist and took an active part in the politics of the day. He learned chemistry from Imam Jafar Sadeq, who was not only a great chemist, but a theologian, as well. Under his patronage and encouragement, Jabir involved himself in the experimental sciences.

Jabir was versatile both in the formulation of theoretical principles and in the practical innovations in the chemistry of his time. It can be said without hesitation that he shifted this branch of knowledge from an art of secrecy and superstition to the realm of science. His contributions in both theoretical and experimental chemistry represent landmarks in scientific development.

Jabir classified minerals and chemicals into three categories:

1. Spirits: Those which sublime on heating such as sulphur, arsenic compounds, mercury, camphor, ammonium salts etc.

2. Metals: Gold, silver, lead, tin, copper, iron, zinc (these correspond to the seven planets then known).

3. Pulverizable Matters: A great variety of substances belong to this category.

According to Jabir, the non-spirit or pulverizable substances, like living objects, are composed of two parts: body and spirits. When body and spirit were mixed in various proportions they gave rise to various substances. Jabir used a theoretical approach to explain the composition of matter. The theory is known as the Sulphur-Mercury Theory. It was quite original, and was postulated when no other theory about this subject existed except the idea of the "four elements" (air, water, fire and earth). It appears that Jabir studied the properties of sulfur from a practical point of view by actual experimentation. It is probable that he formulated the Sulfur-Mercury Theory after a great deal of observations and experimentation. It is for this reason that he is regarded as one of the early innovators in chemistry. Indications of the preparation of sulfur compounds such as cupreous sulfide, black copper sulfide, cinnabar and many other metal sulfides are found in his writings. He prepared the so-called Liver of Sulphur and Milk of Sulphur.

According to Jabir, sulphur may be regarded as the purest form of dry matter and mercury the purest form of wet matter. It was conjectured that the purest form of sulfur and the purest form of mercury, when combined together in the correct proportions, might produce gold. It is obvious that such experiments never succeeded, but they did advance experimental methodology and evolved new techniques to produce new substances. They include a host of new chemicals, some of which have economic value today, such as white lead used as paint, mercury compounds, silver compounds, sulphur compounds, and others. Jabir is also associated with the authorship of a large number of books and treatises, although most of his books appear to have been destroyed during the sack of Baghdad by the Tartars in 1258. Those which still exist in translation, particularly in English, are considered incomplete and distorted. In his book *The Works of Geber*, published in 1928, E. J. Holmyard[11] established that the names "Jabir" and "Geber" were identical and that he was a key figure in the history of the chemical sciences. In his book on Jabir, Paul Kraus attributed about 3000 works to Jabir, dealing not only with alchemy but with many other topics. In 1906, he mentioned the *Books of Seventy* by Geber.[12]

Apart from the discovery of mineral acids and the development of the laboratory, Jabir is credited to have formulated the synthetic processes of a large number of useful substances of commercial importance.

Medical Science

The Greeks introduced a rational approach to medical science and Greek medicine was practiced all over the possessions of the Byzantine (eastern Roman) Empire, western Asia and northern Africa. This was the case when the Prophet Mohammed began his mission in Arabia (610 – 632). The Arabs were generally unaware of Greek medicine at that time, although one Arab, Harith bin Khaldah, was a physician to Kalifah Abu Bakr (the first elected Caliph following the death of Mohammed). The first wave of medical knowledge came to the Islamic world when Muslims made contact with the thoroughly Hellenized Syria and Egypt and the comparatively strongly Hellenized western part of the Sassanid empire. It brought the Muslims in direct contact with alien civilizations, namely, Greek, Roman and Persian. The Jewish, Christians and Sabean physicians practiced Greek medicine, and Muslim conquerors used the service of these non-Muslim physicians. The early Muslims not only conquered new lands and people for their faith, but also were equally enthusiastic in acquiring knowledge. The famous sayings of the Prophet such as

> Search for knowledge even though you might have to travel to China.

> Every disease has its cure.

> The ink of a scholar is more precious than the blood of a martyr.

inspired the Muslims to collect all the books of knowledge of Greek, Egyptian, Persian and even Indian origin and began translating them into Arabic. For about a hundred years, the Muslims translated all the books they encountered, and were aided in this work by non-Muslims, including Jews, Christians, Sabeans, Persians and even few Hindus. From the eighth century, scholars of the Muslim world began to make original contributions in all branches of human knowledge. Soon they became the teachers of the known world and enriched the system of medical science. The Muslims named this system _Unani_ (Ionia of Greece) simply because they started mainly from Greek sources. The Muslims made a unique contribution to the world for they saved the Greek and Egyptian heritage of science from oblivion. The period between the eighth and thirteenth centuries was the golden age of Arab medicine. It was Arab physicians who taught the west _Unani_ medicine, and their writings were part of the curricula in western medical universities into the seventeenth century.

In the Arabic world of the ninth and tenth centuries, the formulation of medical encyclopedias became the standard way of organizing and systematizing the Greek medical knowledge that had passed to the Arabic world via Syria (Edessa), Persia (Nisibis) and Egypt (Alexandria). The Arabic scholars of this period provided an important function of making this medical knowledge available to medical practitioners who needed a simplified compendium of medical theory and medical practice. The first great exponent of a medical compendium was Al-Razi (864 – 93 CE) who was known in the West as Rhazes or Rhazi. He was born in Persia and is considered one of the greatest Muslim physicians of the medieval world. Rhazi is noted for his works on smallpox and measles that were later translated into Latin, English and many other languages. He was considered the most skilled clinician of his time and became a director of hospitals in both his native Persia and later in Baghdad. His skill in prognosis and ability to formulate standardized treatment procedures made him one of the most honored physicians of the Arabic world and (later) of the Latin West. [13] After the fall of Baghdad in 1285 and that of the Western caliphate in 1492, the Muslims began to lag behind the European nations in science and technology. Europeans had already translated Arabic scientific texts into Latin, such as Avicenna's *Canon of Medicine*, which contributed substantially to "learned medicine" in the West. Islamic medical thought built on the original contributions of the Hippocratic tradition and those of Galen, the most noteworthy medical doctor in the ancient world after Hippocrates. Avicenna's *Canon of Medicine* developed a philosophical and scientific methodology for determining the causes of illness and the methods for restoring health to the patient. His analysis of the mental and emotional states that can cause illness provided the foundation for what today is called mind/body medicine or holistic medicine.

---

[1] Seyyed Hossein Nasr, *Science and Civilization in Islam* (Chicago: ABC International Group, 2001), 176.

[2] Ibid., 172.

[3] Arthur Koestler, *The Sleepwalkers: A History of Man's Changing Vision of the Universe*, (London: Hutchinson and Co., 1959).

[4] Victor Roberts, "The Solar and Lunar Theory of Ibn ash-Shatir: A Pre-Copernican Copernican Model," Isis 48, (1957): 428 – 432.

[5] W. W. Rouse Ball, *A Short History of Mathematics* (New York: Dover, 1960), 158.

[6] Ibid., 158.

[7] Ibid., 158. Sami Ibrahim of San Jose City College pointed out to me the importance of Arab mathematics for the scientific enterprise of the West. In addition to astronomy, Arab/Muslim mathematicians and scientists used algebra and trigonometry for navigation and architecture. The Arabs loved Euclidean geometry but they also introduced spherical geometry into their calculations and writings. Much of this knowledge passed to the West during the later Middle Ages.

[8] For Ptolemaic astronomy in Islam, see David C. Lindberg, *The Beginnings of Western Science: The European Scientific Tradition in Philosophical, Religious, and Institutional Context, 600 B.C. to A.D. 1450* (Chicago: University of Chicago Press, 1992), 177.

[9] See *History of Islamic Science*, http://www.levity.com/alchemy/islam14.html.

[10] David C. Lindberg, *The Beginnings of Western Science* (Chicago: University of Chicago Press, 1992). 287 – 290.

[11] E. J. Holmyard, The Works of Geber (Kila, MT: Kessinger Publishing, reprinted 1942). This may be found at www.amazon.com.

[12] Paul Kraus, "Jâbir ibn Hayyân: Contributions à l'Historie des Ideés Scientifiques dan l'Islam II: Jâbor et la Science Grecque," *Mémories de l'Institut d'Égypte* 45, 1 (1942).

[13] Gerald Grudzen, Ph. D. *Monte Cassino and Medical Philosophy: Body and Soul Dilemmas.* Ph. D Dissertation (NY: Columbia University, 2006), 256.

Discussion Questions

1) What were some of the key Muslim contributions to astronomy during the Middle Ages?

2) What was the relationship of astronomy to the Muslim faith during the Middle Ages?

3) What contributions did Muslims make to the chemical sciences?

4) How did Muslims incorporate the medical sciences into their culture?

5) What role did members of the Jewish and Christian traditions play in the medical sciences within the Islamic culture?

Chapter Seven

Spirituality and Science in the Modern World

Gerald Grudzen, PhD

Many scholars of western civilization date the beginning of the modern era with the historical period of the Renaissance and Reformation in the West. The Renaissance focused on the humanistic values which we find expressed most eloquently in the works of Desiderius Erasmus (1466-1536) such as his *Praise of Folly* (1515) which attacked many of the "follies" or corrupt practices found within the structures of Catholicism, particularly within monasticism. Even though Erasmus never separated himself from the Roman Catholic Church, his satire on the prevalent abuses within the church paved the way for the attack of Martin Luther (1483-1546) on the promulgation and sale of church indulgences. Luther attached 96 theses to the church door at Wittenberg in 1517 which were welcomed by many of the humanists who espoused church reforms such as Erasmus had promoted just a few years earlier. Luther was summoned to the Diet of Worms in 1521 where he refused to recant his positions about indulgences, celibacy of the clergy, pilgrimages and religious orders. Luther also produced a German translation of the Bible which became a central part of the German Reformation tradition. Luther and his fellow Reformers, Huldrych Zwingli (1484-1531) and John Calvin (1509-1564) were linked with the views of the Renaissance humanists and rejected the natural theology of the scholastic era in favor of a more intimate and devotional faith based upon biblical moral principles."Zwingli and Calvin, indeed, remained humanists throughout their lives, their religious reform largely inspired by the Renaissance zeitgeist." [1]

The Renaissance humanists cared greatly about the translation of classic texts from the Greek and Roman era and focused mostly on works of poetry, grammar, rhetoric and history. Cicero became the model writer of humanistic discourses. Cicero's rhetorical style was quite different from that of the medieval scholastic philosophers and theologians. Cicero's moral philosophy such as found in his *On Duties* and *Tusculan Disputation* were particularly popular among the Renaissance humanists. "From Petrarch's time onward, when professional humanist took any interest at all in philosophy, they nearly always concerned themselves with ethical questions….Throughout the fifteenth and early sixteenth centuries, condemnation of scholastic university education was the ceaseless hue and cry of the humanists.[2] In the world of art the fifteenth century also marked a break with the past and the beginning of the linear perspective in art emphasizing a more naturalistic understanding of the human form. Even though the Renaissance had a Platonic dimension with its search for the ideal form of beauty, there was also a scientific dimension that we find particularly notable in both Michelangelo and Leonardo.

Luther represented a turning point in the history of western civilization from a more communal spirituality represented by the monastic life which had permeated so much of western piety until the Reformation era to a more individualistic and worldly spirituality. The quest for religious certainty began to take over the popular mentality in the modern era and the search for such certainly became the leitmotif for Luther himself. "But the new emphasis on the individual made Luther so obsessed with his own spiritual performance that he had become mired in the ego that he was supposed to transcend ... In addition he had expressed the yearning for absolute certainty that would characterized religion in the modern period." [3]

Luther had studied the philosophy and theology of William of Ockham, which emphasized the absolute and omnipotent power of God that transcended all earthly signs of God's presence in nature. Luther's "deliberate desacralization of the cosmos was a secularizing idea that would encourage scientists to approach the world independently of the divine." [4]

Luther's revolution not only affected the reorganization of the Christian church but it also brought about a change in the popular culture of modernity. Charles Taylor has examined the emergence of the secular culture in modernity and found that it represents a split between an elite and popular culture. According to Taylor, "Popular modes of piety (in the Middle Ages), for instance, were shared by gentry and clergy, everyone participated in Carnival." [5]

The development of "elites" became part of the process of transformation that led to the reconstruction of philosophy, theology and science in the modern era. According to the ancient ethical ideals of Plato, Aristotle and the Stoics, "the dominant image of virtue was that of the soul in harmony. The master idea was of a form which was already at work in human nature, which the virtuous person has to help emerge, rather than a pattern imposed ab extra (from outside)." [6]

We see then the beginning of a shift from a more contemplative understanding of nature to one in which we attempt to control or shape nature. "The Renaissance gave an important role in this respect to the artist. "Marsilio Ficino expressed this idea: "the human person imitates all the works of divine nature; those of inferior nature he brings to perfection, corrects, and improves." ....Michelangelo saw himself as working in this way. Leonardo sees that the artist must submit to the "ragioni" (reason) that we find in nature, but our task must be to bring these out fully through our own rational and constructive activity." [7]

Francis Bacon (1561-1626) took the emphasis upon practical or instrumental reason to another level when he attempted to replace the largely deductive logic of Aristotle with that of his own inductive method expressed in his *Novum Organon (New Instrument)* in 1620. Bacon's empiricist philosophy was based largely upon an enumerative inductive method, which he felt would lead to practical benefits for humanity through the growth of scientific and technological innovations. Bacon's "instrumental" reason stands in contrast to the contemplative and mystical traditions of the monotheistic religions. Just as Luther claimed that every believer had direct access to God so Bacon asserted that every person, even without prior formal education, could arrive at inductive truth as long as he or she used the proper inductive instrument in observation of facts leading to generalizations in the form of scientific laws. "Francis Bacon offers us an insight into the tremendous excitement and optimism that reverberated throughout the Renaissance and accompanied the rise of modern science... The result for this extraordinary optimism was that the scientific method was like a machine into which we pour the data of nature and receive scientific laws out the other end. "[8]Bacon's approach to the inductive, scientific method had severe limitations because he lacked a sophisticated understanding of Galileo's accomplishments and he rejected the Copernican heliocentric theory that became the centerpiece of the Scientific Revolution. "In spite of his shortcomings, Bacon's contributions to the history of philosophy is threefold: (1) he was an early leader in the empiricist movement, (2) he was a pioneer in the attempt to systematize the scientific method, and (3) he was the founder of the modern inductive logic." [9]

Bacon marked the turning point away from the Aristotelian approach to the scientific method that had been part of the scholastic method since the birth of the medieval universities in the eleventh and twelfth centuries when Aristotle's works were recovered in the West. The rejection of Aristotle's deductive logic and the new quest for certitude in epistemology brought about the dualism we see reflected in the Method of Doubt found in the writings of Descartes. Both Galileo and Descartes relied upon quantitative rather qualitative measures to fathom the properties of nature. Aristotle had also emphasized teleology in his philosophical method and claimed that purpose or final causality was built into nature.

> In sharp contrast, according to Galileo and Descartes, the study of nature should concern itself with the measureable properties of nature, such as size, shape, and motion. This put all natural things on the same level, subject to the same mathematical physical laws, and it means that natural objects differ only in quantitative ways. This, in turn, implied the rejection of Aristotle's four elements, earth, water, air and fire, and the denial of his distinction between the lower earthly and the higher celestial levels.[10]

The medieval view of the cosmos reflected an organic and sacramental vision of the physical universe in which the presence of the divine manifested itself in the regular processes of nature such as the seasons of the year and the movement of the heavenly spheres. The Scientific Revolution led by Galileo, Descartes and Bacon seemed to separate the material and spiritual worlds. Science would now focus only on the material and physical dimension of nature and the role of religion and spirituality was purely in the internal workings of the mind. Descartes' renewal of Anselm's Ontological proof for God's existence acted as a template for the new attempt to fashion a rational proof for God's presence but it lacked any direct connection with the material realm of nature. All three of the monotheistic religions had relied upon nature to provide access to signs of the Creator's imprint even though they each had different approaches based upon their interpretation of the revelations found in the Hebrew Bible, the New Testament and the Qur'an. Each of the monotheistic religions had developed a theology of nature even though none of them believed that God's nature could be accessible or knowable by human reason. Aquinas only held to demonstrable proof for God's existence but God's nature was only revealed through revelation. For this reason nature would, by necessity, need to be open to the divine action and not closed to it otherwise revelation and divine action in the world would be impossible.

A mew understanding of nature began to take hold in the West during the period of the Enlightenment most notably influenced by the mechanistic science and philosophy of Sir Isaac Newton. (1642-1727)

> Newton achieved a magnificent synthesis that brought together in a single theory Cartesian physics, Kepler's law of planetary motion, and Galileo's law of terrestrial movement.....Everything – the annual orbits of the planets, the rotation of the earth, the motions of the moon, the tidal movements of the seas, the precession of the equinox, a stone falling to the ground – could now be explained by gravity. Gravity caused all bodies to incline mutually toward one another; it preserved the planets from flying off into space and enabled them to maintain their stable orbits at the relative speeds and distances specified by Kepler.[11]

Since Newton believed that matter was inert and lifeless, the movement of the planets and the earth itself could not be explained by the laws of gravity. According to Newton, following a form of thought going back to Aristotle and Thomas Aquinas, the world could not be fully understood without the assumption of a First Cause.

> The main Business of natural Philosophy is to argue from Phaenomena without feigning Hypothesis; and to deduce Causes from Effects, till we come to the very first Cause, which certainly is not mechanical; and not only to unfold the Mechanism of the World, but chiefly to resolve these and such like Questions.[12]

Newton believed that the "primordial faith" came about prior to the birth of the monotheistic religions and it was based on a rational understanding of nature. "Scientific rationalism, therefore, was what Newton called the "fundamental religion." But it had been corrupted with "Monstrous Legends, false miracles, veneration of reliques, charmes, ye doctrine of Ghosts or Daemons, and their Intercession, invocations and worship and other such heathen superstitions." [13] Newton's _Philosophia Naturalis Principia Mathematica_ (1687) had revolutionized the modern understanding of the universe as no longer operating under separate principles for the earth and the heavens above. The earth and heavens could not only be understood by human reason using the principles of the new mathematics but it could lead to man's dominion over nature through technological innovations, which would characterize the Industrial Revolution that took hold first in Great Britain. Alexander Pope eulogized Newton when he said:

> Nature and Nature's laws lay hid in night
> Go said, let Newton be! and all was Light.[14]

John Locke (1632-1705) popularized the Enlightenment philosophy and he helped to spread the "Gospel" of Deism, a natural philosophy of religion inspired by Newtonian science and the empirical philosophy developed by Locke's "representative realism." Locke's philosophy placed a separation between the object of knowledge and the knowing subject. Locke rejected the Platonic assumption that there were innate ideas in favor of his assumption that the mind was a "tabula rasa" or "blank slate." Locke became one of the most important promoters of the new philosophy of religion known as Deism. Locke had written an _Essay on Reasonableness of Christianity_ (1695) that denied God would intervene in the world either through a divine revelation or in the form of a miracle. According to Locke "The world is a self-sufficient, rational system that runs according to divinely created natural laws...." [15] Locke and Newton's influence spread dramatically to the British colonies in the Americas and were reflected in the thought and writings of many of the leading figures in the American revolution. Benjamin Franklin (1706-1790) and Thomas Jefferson (1743-1826) were two of the leading figures in the American colonies who promoted the Deist philosophy of the Enlightenment. "Inspired by Newton's vision of a universe ruled by immutable laws, they were offended by a God who intervened erratically in nature, working miracles and revealing "mysteries" that were not accessible to our reasoning powers." [16] The Enlightenment reflected a process that had begun with the discoveries of Copernicus and Galileo which transformed the narrative about the place of the earth in the universe and led also to the rejection of the Aristotelian and scholastic synthesis of Faith and Reason which the Catholic Church had embraced through the masterful writings of Thomas Aquinas. Descartes' Method of Doubt led to a separation of body and soul, matter and spirit which led to an understanding of the material universe as ruled by mechanistic and mathematical laws discovered so brilliantly by Sir Isaac Newton.

> The Enlightenment was the culmination of a vision that had been long in the making. It built on Galileo's mechanistic science, Descartes' quest for autonomous certainty, and Newton's cosmic laws, aided by the eighteenth century, the philosophes believed that they had acquired a uniform way of assessing the whole of reality. Reason was the only path to truth.[17]

One of the other key figures in the revolutionary era was Thomas Paine (1737-1809). Paine ascribed intently and fervently to the Deist philosophy and wrote his own philosophical tract about its impact entitled *The Age of Reason* (1794). In the opening paragraph Paine sets forth his views, addressed to his "fellow citizens of the United States of American" that Reason should be the ultimate guide in evaluating religious truths.

I PUT the following work under your protection. It contains my opinions upon Religion. You will do me the justice to remember, that I have always strenuously supported the Right of every Man to his own opinion, however different that opinion might be to mine. He who denies to another this right, makes a slave of himself to his present opinion, because he precludes himself the right of changing it. The most formidable weapon against errors of every kind is Reason. I have never used any other, and I trust I never shall.[18]

In the first section of *The Age of Reason* Paine initially states his own beliefs: "I believe in one God, and no more; and I hope for happiness beyond this life. I believe in the equality of man; and I believe that religious duties consist in doing justice, loving mercy, and endeavoring to make our fellow-creatures happy." [19] Following the statement of his own creed, Paine states that he does not believe in the creeds of the established religions with which he was familiar.

I do not believe in the creed professed by the Jewish church, by the Roman church, by the Greek church, by the Turkish church, by the Protestant church, nor by any church that I know of. My own mind is my own church. All national institutions of churches, whether Jewish, Christian or Turkish, appear to me no other than human inventions, set up to terrify and enslave mankind, and monopolize power and profit.[20]

It is clear that Paine identifies Islam with the "Turkish Church" and claims that each of the major Religions can be called a "church" since that was the form of religious organization with which he was familiar. Paine does affirm the existence of God as First Cause based upon his own use of Reason which he claims is the only sure path to affirm the existence of a single supreme being.

He rejects all religious institutions and states that his own mind "is my own church."

> It is only by the exercise of reason that man can discover God. Take away that reason, and he would be incapable of understanding anything; and, in this case, it would be just as consistent to read even the book called the Bible to a horse as to a man. How, then, is it that those people pretend to reject reason? Almost the only parts in the book called the Bible that convey to us any idea of God, are some chapters in Job and the 19th Psalm; I recollect no other. Those parts are true deistical compositions, for they treat of the Deity through his works. They take the book of Creation as the word of God, they refer to no other book, and all the inferences they make are drawn from that volume.[21]

Paine was the first of the Founding Fathers to advocate the abolition of slavery in 1775. In an essay written to the Pennsylvania Journal and the Weekly Advertise Paine attacked any justification for the slave trade in the American colonies.

> That some desperate wretches should be willing to steal and enslave men by violence and murder for gain, is rather lamentable than strange. But that many civilized, nay, Christianized people should approve, and be concerned in the savage practice, is surprising; and still persist, though it has been so often proved contrary to the light of nature, to every principle of Justice and Humanity, and even good policy, by a succession of eminent men, and several late publications. Our Traders in MEN (an unnatural commodity!) must know the wickedness of the SLAVE-TRADE, if they attend to reasoning, or the dictates of their own hearts: and such as shun and stiffle all these, wilfully sacrifice Conscience, and the character of integrity to that golden idol.[22]

Part of the reason for the growing disjunction between religion and science in the modern era could be attributed to the failure of religious institutions to live up to the high moral ideals found within their founding sacred texts and the example of their founders. Paine was also one of the leaders in promoting religious toleration which had become another facet of the Enlightenment philosophy.

"I do not mean by this declaration to condemn those who believe otherwise; they have the same right to their belief as I have to mine. But it is necessary to the happiness of man, that he be mentally faithful to himself. Infidelity does not consist in believing, or in disbelieving; it consists in professing to believe what he does not believe".[23]

The Enlightenment played a pivotal role in the further weakening of the image of organized religion among the educated classes both in Europe and in the United States. Thomas Jefferson, the leading Enlightenment figure among the Founding Fathers of the United States, became a pioneer in establishing public higher education in the United States. He founded the University of Virginia, the first publicly supported university in the United States and dedicated to educating civic leaders and free of control by any religious body. Jefferson espoused the Deist philosophy and removed all the miracles from his copy of the New Testament. Jefferson's true passion seemed to be the pursuit of scientific investigations.

> Jefferson wished he could be a scientist all the time. When he was leaving the presidency in early 1809, he wrote, "Nature intended me for the tranquil pursuits of science, by rendering them my supreme delight." In fact, do you know what Jefferson did during the week in 1797 when he became vice president of the United States? He presented a formal research paper on paleontology to his scientific colleagues in the American Philosophical Society! Paleontology is the study of fossils. It helps us understand all the Earth's forms of

life.Jefferson also helped invent modern agricultural science and technology. He believed agriculture was the most important science. By himself, he re-engineered the plow according to scientific principles that came from Sir Isaac Newton, the inventor of mathematical physics. Re-inventing the plow may sound boring. But ask yourself: In Jefferson's time, what technological devices were more important than the plow?[24]

Jefferson's enthusiasm for the natural and human sciences as well as his dedication to public education would become two of the most powerful themes leading to the growth of the United States as the leader of the western world in the following two centuries. It would also, however, lead to the privatization of religious experience and the growth of an empiricism as the only way to understand the nature of religious experience.

Paine's naturalistic religion and that of other Enlightenment thinkers led to another popular form of thought in the nineteenth century in the United States known as Transcendentalism. The key leaders in this movement, Ralph Waldo Emerson (1803-1882) on and Henry David Thoreau (1817-1862) , stressed the power of the individual and the need for social reform. They were among the first to lead in the cause of equality for women and the abolition of slavery. They did not share Paine's unfettered belief in reason since it had led to the oppressive forces found in the Industrial Revolution.They did share a desire for social reform but this was generally outside the scope of organized religious institutions.

As a group, the transcendentalists led the celebration of the American experiment as one of individualism and self-reliance. They took progressive stands on women's rights, abolition, reform, and education. They criticized government, organized religion, laws, social institutions, and creeping industrialization. They created an American "state of mind" in which imagination was better than reason, creativity was better than theory, and action was better than contemplation. And they had faith that all would be well because humans could transcend limits and reach astonishing heights[25]

William James, MD, (1842-1910) studied religion from the standpoint of empirical science and his approach became the standard method for understanding the epistemological scope of religious experience from the end of the twentieth century to the present time. His classical study of religious experience, *The Varieties of Religious Experience: A Study of Human Nature* (1902), became the standard approach to religious studies used in most American colleges and universities. James was also one of the early pioneers in the study of Psychology and wrote one of the first textbooks in Psychology, *Principles of Psychology* ((1890) while a professor at Harvard University. In his *Varieties of Religious Experience* James presented his pragmatic philosophy of religion. For James a belief was "true" insofar as it had positive psychological and moral results for the individual and the community in which he or she lived. James was attempting to move beyond the Kantian dualism, which divided phenomenal reality known through sense experience and religious experience which claimed to access God or the supernatural through such a noumenal "object," which was beyond the reach of empirical science. With James' pragmatic philosophy of religious experience, the quality of religious experience could be determined by the results it produced in the individual believer. In his famous debate with W.K. Clifford documented in his essay *The Will to Believe* (1897), James distinguishes between various kinds of options, the existence of God being one in which the consequences are momentous. The decision that a person takes about the existence of God is, for James, a forced option. Not making a decision about God's existence is a decision in itself. James' opponent on this matter was the philosopher W.K. Clifford who held that religious belief was unjustified and even could be considered immoral because there was no rational or empirical evidence to justify belief in God.

It would be the same as telling someone to believe in the tooth fairy or Santa Claus. James' argument was that the grounds for belief are based on pragmatic principles:

> Since James, like David Hume, doesn't think that rational arguments for or against God's existence are persuasive, the grounds for belief are to be found in practical considerations. "On pragmatic principles, if the hypothesis of God works satisfactorily in the widest sense of the word, it is true." [26]

The attacks against traditional religion in Europe took a radical turn toward the middle of the nineteenth century with the publication of Ludwig Feuerbach's *The Essence of Christianity* (1841). The "God" of Hegel's philosophy, the Absolute Spirit, had brought God down into the processes of human history and culture. God could not be found within such a human construct according to critics of Hegelianism. "So man's belief in God is nothing other than his own being."[27]

Karl Marx (1818-1883) would transform Hegel's philosophy and claim that religion was only an "opiate" to deaden the human spirit in the face of oppression by the owners of industry who controlled the major economic forces of a capitalist society, the means of production. According to Marx's *Communist Manifesto* (1849) and *Das Kapital* (1867) the science of economics could lead humanity to a brave new world of equality and mutual ownership of social goods. Marx, like Hagel, was relying upon a deterministic understanding of empirical science to reveal what he felt were the inevitable historical laws that would bring about the collapse of capitalism. The impact of the philosophy of Marx would be felt over the entire course of the twentieth century particularly in eastern Europe, China and Latin America. Part of the reason for the attack upon Christianity by Feuerbach and Marx lay in the identification of Christianity with the European colonial powers who had spread their imperial

Gospel to the Americas, India and Africa over the course of the eighteenth and nineteenth centuries.

The seeming triumph of western culture in much of the developing world could be attributed o the growing influence of a professional scientific class of well educated professionals who 'used their scientific and mathematical skills to create the industrial and later the digital civilization found in the West and then spread it throughout the world by the beginning of the twenty first century.

The impact of western science and technology did not go unnoticed in the many parts of the developing world, particularly those with large Muslim populations. One of the key figures in the dialogue between the Islamic faith and the emerging scientific culture of the West was Sir Sayid Ahmed Khan (1817-1898), a Muslim philosopher and educator who was born into the Mughal nobility of India but became one of the leading social reformers of nineteenth century India and in considered one of the founding fathers of the nation of Pakistan. Sir Sayid was also the founder of the Algarth School in 1877 (aka known later as Algarth Muslim University) which attempted to unite traditional Islamic values and traditions with a modern, scientific and progressing education. "Sir Sayid was convinced that that if he could shine the light of European rationalism and scientific thought upon traditional Muslim beliefs and customs, the results would be an indigenous Islamic Enlightenment that would propel the Muslim world into the twentieth century."[28] Sir Sayid hoped to free the education of Muslims from its control by the Ulama (Islamic legal scholars) and thus bring about a modernization of the Islamic understanding of the Shariah (Islamic legal codes). A contemporary effort similar to that of Sir Sayid has been inspired by the Turkish scholar and mystic, Fethullah Gulen, founder of the Gulen Movmement which sponsors educational institutions in over 100 countries with a focus on universal values and math and science education. [29] Perhaps no event was more emblematic of the shift occurring in the relationship of science and religion was the publication of Charles Darwin's *Origin of the Species by Means of Natural Selection* in 1859. "Later in the *Descent of Man* (1871), he suggested even more controversially that Homo Sapiens had developed from the progenitor of the orangutan, gorilla and chimpanzee. Human beings were not the pinnacle of purposeful creation; like everything else they had evolved by trial and error, and God had had no direct hand in their making."[30]

Prior to the publication of Darwin's writings most western Christians either accepted the biblical account of creation as found in Genesis or they were willing to accept a rational explanation of the universe utilizing the arguments of natural theology in which God was the Grand Designer of the Universe and that his "fingerprints" could be discerned in the workings of nature. "Darwin's discoveries accelerated the already growing tendency to exclude theology from scientific discussion....Wholly dependent on concrete, measureable fact, science now rejected any hypothesis that was not based on the human experience of the natural world and could not, therefore, be tested." [31]

Biblical "Higher Criticism," first developed at German universities, gradually spread to the other parts of Europe and then to the United States. The trend toward "demythologizing" the Bible had taken hold in many parts of the Protestant world with biblical scholars such as Rudolph Bultmann relying more on existential philosophy than a traditional theological paradigm of fides quaerens intellectum – faith seeking understanding. By the end of the nineteenth century a conservative backlash against the biblical Higher Criticism began to emerge with the growth of biblical fundamentalism and Protestant Evangelism as antidotes to the growing influence of the Higher Criticism in university based religion departments and liberal Protestant seminaries such as Union Theological Seminary in New York. The Catholic Church did not embrace the new biblical criticism until much later in the twentieth century when Pope Pius Xii issued the encyclical, *Divino Afflante Spiritu*, in 1943. In this encyclical Pius XiI embraced the scientific study of the Scriptures using the tools provided by linguists who were familiar with the ancient biblical languages of Hebrew and Greek. Biblical archeology, literary scholarship which specialized in comparative study of literary forms called "form criticism," and the history of ancient cultures in which the books of the Bible came to be written all contributed to the growth of scientific biblical studies. Until the publication of *Divino Afflante Spiritu* the Catholic Church had relied upon the Latin Vulgate translation of Saint Jerome completed about 400 AD. Pius XII realized that the Church needed to embrace the new biblical sciences which provided many valuable insights into the clarity and meaning of sacred texts.

> In the present day indeed this art, which is called textual criticism and which is used with great and praiseworthy results in the editions of profane writings, is also quite rightly employed in the case of the Sacred Books, because of that very reverence which is due to the Divine Oracles. For its very purpose is to insure that the sacred text be restored, as perfectly as possible, be purified from the corruptions due to the carelessness of the copyists and be freed, as far as may be done, from glosses and omissions, from the interchange and repetition of words and from all other kinds of mistakes, which are wont to make their way gradually into writings handed down through many centuries.[32]

This encyclical provided a method for integrating secular and sacred "sciences" which allowed Catholic biblical scholars to undertake rigorous preparation for the work of translating sacred texts using the latest methods and techniques found in the study of other ancient texts, cultures and civilizations other than those found within the biblical canon. A new English version of the Jerusalem Bible, first published in 1966, became the first new version of the Bible based upon ancient Hebrew and Greek sources since the publication of the Latin Vulgate by St. Jerome at the end of the fourth century CE. This version had been made the official version of the Catholic Church at the Council of Trent (1545-1563) and remained such until the middle of the twentieth century.

At about the same time that Pius XII was issuing his encyclical on the Sacred Scriptures the Vatican was blocking the publication of the writings of the Jesuit priest and scientific scholar, Teilhard de Chardin (1881-1955). Chardin had written extensively about the possible relationship of evolutionary science with a spirituality of the earth and the cosmos in *The Phenomenon of Man* (1955) This book was published posthumously after Teilhard de Chardin's death earlier that year. Chardin had done extensive paleontological research in China and was well recognized as a scholar in the field of evolutionary research. Teilhard developed a threefold theory of evolution that begins with what he called the Geosphere, the period of evolution prior to the birth of life but within which the basis for life is formed in the galaxies and planet earth; the second period of evolution is known as the Biosphere, the era in which the various physical life forms come into being and which lead to the "ascent" of homo sapiens. Teilhard called the final phase of evolution in which we now reside the Noosphere, the formation of a thought envelope circling planet earth. In his understanding of the human phenomena Teilhard moved beyond the mechanistic and materialistic views that had characterized much of the popular understanding of evolutionary science.

> Science is necessarily chiefly concerned with studying the material arrangements that are successively effected by the progress of life. In so doing, it sees only the outer crust of things. The true evolution of the world takes place in souls and in their union. Its inner factors are not mechanistic but psychological and moral. That, as we shall again have occasion to note, is why the further, physical development of humankind – the true communion, that is, of its planetary, biological evolution – will be found in the increased consciousness obtained by the psychical forces of unification. [33]

Teilhard projected the eventual unity of humanity in what he called the Omega Point. For Teilhard this point of unification coincided with what Christian historical theology called the Pleroma or the culmination of history with the perfection of the cosmos as a completely Divine Milieu, also the title of Teilhard's spirituality of the material universe. Unlike Descartes, Teilhard did not separate matter and spirit or the mind and the body. He claimed that the material world has been transformed by the "omnipresence" of the divine.

> However vast the divine milieu may be, it is in reality a center. It therefore has the properties of a center and above all the absolute and final power to unite (and consequently to complete) all beings within its breast. In the divine milieu all the elements of the universe touch each other by that which is most inward and ultimate in them. There they concentrate, little by little, all that is purest and most attractive in them without loss and without danger of subsequent corruption.[34]

Teilhard's mystical vision of a humanity headed toward a unified consciousness seems, to many, highly unlikely if not impossibly quixotic. Nevertheless, the pace of technological revolutions, particularly the birth and development of the Internet and new modes of instantaneous communication throughout the globe enable some to view Teilhard as the prophet of the future destiny of humankind. Other prophets of the future such as Martin Luther King, Nelson Mandela and Maya Angelou struggled to find their voice despite powerful forces opposing them but eventually their message became part of the present reality and not just a future dream.

Spirituality and science are two of the melodies constantly playing now in the contemporary world with each claiming its own phalanx of followers defending the authority of their position as guardians of either science or spirituality. Stephen Jay Gould (1941-2002) one of the foremost evolutionary biologists on the past century, wrote extensively on religion and science and developed the theory of NOMA, "non-overlapping magisterium." Gould held that religion and science represented two completely different domains of knowledge. "The realm of science, according to Gould, is that of "factual knowledge," and that of religions is "values and meaning." [35] For Gould religion does not put us in touch with any objective reality beyond what we perceive to be subjectively real for us. This kind of epistemological stance leads to various forms of philosophical relativism in which all forms of belief are lumped together as relative either to a particular culture or a particular religious tradition. The determinism found in traditional mechanistic interpretations of science led to the Deist model of religion which became part of the Enlightenment. The developments that have occurred in the world o contemporary science have opened up the scientific method to the realm of chance and unpredictability. "Unlike the science of the Enlightenment period, which envisioned the universe operating in a determined, mechanistic way, today's science has revealed the existence of extensive zones of openness in nature. In these areas where what happens next is intrinsically unpredictable."[36] The emergent view of evolution holds that we, homo sapiens, are an active agent in the evolutionary process and not simply a deterministic product of natural selection or genetic mapping.

> Most students of evolution continue to believe, contrary to Dawkins, that it is the organism that evolves, not just the genes. Mary Jane West-Eberhard emphasizes the role of the organism (phenotypes) in its own evolution: "I consider genes followers, not leaders, in adaptive evolution." ....Of particular importance are the behavioral and symbolic aspects of evolution, which build on genetic capacities but are themselves not genetically controlled, as it is there that we will probably find most of the resources for religion -- cultural developments from biological beginnings.[37]

Richard Dawkins, the noted evolutionary biologist at Oxford University, is best known for his book *The God Delusion* (2006). Dawkins builds most of his own philosophy on the theory that evolutionary biology is sufficient to explain the emergence of homo sapiens and nothing external to it such as a supernatural order is necessary to explain how we developed our present forms of biological and human life. Dawkins fails to understand that religion and science each are based upon symbolic systems of thought each with their own internal structures and method of arriving at "objective" truth. Both science and religion depend upon what Robert Bellah calls "symbolic transcendence."

> Without the capacity for symbolic transcendence, for seeing the realm of daily life in terms of a realm beyond it, without the capacity for "beyonding" as Kenneth Burke puts it, one would be trapped in a world of what has been called dreadful immanence. For the world of daily life seen solely as a world of rational response to anxiety and need is a world of mechanical necessity, not radical autonomy. It is through pointing to other realities, through beyonding, that religion and poetry, and science too in its own way, break the dreadful fatalities of this world of appearances.[38]

The ability of human beings to project their consciousness beyond the established order of their culture and surroundings can be considered part of the basis for both science and religion. Each of the founders of the great religious traditions such as Jesus, Mohammad and Buddha could look beyond the inherited structures of their religions systems and find new ways to imagine the meaning behind those systems but also inspire disciples who could create rituals and symbolic systems to allow those traditions to grow and evolve. In a somewhat similar manner scientific ingenuity relies upon a variety of theoretical assumptions about reality that cannot be "seen" immediately in everyday life. Science cannot literally "see" the Big Bang; it is a kind of metaphor or analogy for what we know about the origin of the universe from the latest studies and theories assembled by teams of scientists around the world. Just as religion has evolved in the modern world to claim new insights into the person of Jesus through the work of historians associated with the "historical Jesus" research studies,[39] so also has our understanding of cosmology and the evolving universe broadened ad deepened over the past century. Only in recent times have we begun to understand the age of the physical universe, about 13.7 billion years, and the event which initiated our spatial and temporal universe known today as the "Big Bang." Recent discoveries of the radiation coming from this seminal event have led to various theories about how it did occur and within what amount of time that it happened. A flurry of scientific dialogue has surrounded a recent study led by John Kovac of Harvard which seemed to confirm the origin of the universe in what is known as the inflation theory first proposed by Professor Alan Guth of Stanford University in 1979.

> Reaching back across 13.8 billion years to *the first sliver of cosmic time* with telescopes at the South Pole, a team of astronomers led by John M. Kovac of the Harvard-Smithsonian Center for Astrophysics detected ripples in the fabric of space-time — so- called gravitational waves — the signature of a universe being wrenched violently apart when it was roughly a trillionth of a trillionth of a trillionth of a second old. They are the long-sought smoking-gun evidence of inflation, proof, Dr. Kovac and his colleagues say, that Dr. Guth was correct. Inflation has been the workhorse of cosmology for 35 years, though many, including Dr. Guth, wondered whether it could ever be proved.[40]

After the initial excitement of this discovery seeming to "prove" the inflation theory, other cosmologists came forward with an alternative theory that the results of the study of the Kovac's team of scientists might have been compromised by cosmic dust which would "cloud" the findings about the inflation theory of the Big Bang. The skepticism of some scientists did not seem to alter the general belief among cosmologists that the inflation theory would eventually be accepted as the best explanation available for the Big Bang. The science of cosmology generally must deal with questions about the origin of the universe within the realm of probability rather than certainty. In some ways we can see that the studies about the historical Jesus by contemporary scholars must also deal with probable narratives that fit into the existing documentation available to us such as the New Testament and a few other historical documents such as the *The Jewish Antiquities* by Flavius Josephus. Both scientists and religious scholars will often debate about their interpretation of the available evidence which usually is not conclusive. The idea of "certainty" either in science or religion often leads to dogmatic positions which claim some type of "infallibility." Many of the conflicts in the religion and science dialogue are often epistemological and ontological in nature and not purely "scientific."

The New York Times has featured a series of interviews about religion and science entitled The Stone and chaired by Doctor Gary Cutting, a Professor of Philosophy at the University of Notre Dame. The seventh in a series of interviews featured a dialogue with Tim Maudlin, a professor of philosophy at New York University. One of the questions that arose in the interview revolved around the anthropic principle or whether the universe seemed to be designed in such a way to allow life to be possible and to flourish. In the interview with Professor Tim Maudlin, Professor Cutting referred to this principle as the "fine tuning" of physical constants. [41] Professor Maudlin rejects the "fine tuning" argument or the existence of a "fine tuner" such as the monotheistic deity by stating that "If there were some deity who desired that we know of its existence, there would be simple, clear ways to convey that information. I would say that any theistic argument that starts with the constants of nature cannot end with deity who is interested n us knowing of its existence." [42] According to Maudlin, "Atheism is the default position in any scientific inquiry – As yet, there is no direct experimental evidence of a deity ..." [43]

Mehdi Golshani, an Iranian physicist and a leading figure in the dialogue between Islam and science, claims that "the investigation of the physical world cannot dispense with interpretive elements and concepts that are not to be directly encountered in the very physical realm ....Empiricism is thus the philosophy for science, but the wrong one for Goshani. In the same manner, Goshani lists the usage of biological evolution to support atheism among the "wrong" philosophical interpretations for natural science."[44] Goshani accepts the scientific method in the modern world as well established now and that it would be inappropriate to attempt to find scientific discoveries, for example, in the Qur'an. "This kind of exegetical exercise, according to Goshani, incorrectly reduces the Qur'an to a repository of scientific notions -- an "encyclopedia," as opposed to a book of guidance."[45] According to Goshani and other Christian scientists and philosophers, science must be rooted In metaphysical and ontological knowledge which is just as real as that of the empirical presupposition of modern science.

> "At the core of the Islamic metaphysical outlook on science, according to Goshani, is the principle of divine unity or al-tawhid through which the researcher can see the "Interrelation" and "common origin" of the different phenomena of the universe. In this way, the Qur'an provides the researcher with a theistic antidote to hyperspecialization.... If one embraces the Islamic outlook, in Goshani's view, science is practiced as an act of worship and becomes a "ladder to God" while nature is seen as God's handiwork, and respected as such.[46]

Goshani's philosophical viewpoint is remarkably similar to that of Thomas Aquinas and the Neo-Scholastic tradition in the philosophy of moderate realism. According to Thomas, following somewhat in the tradition of Aristotle, the physical universe is not self explanatory and requires some form of teleological explanation which transcends purely empirical forms of reasoning as developed within the hypothetical, theoretical and inductive models employed by modern science. One of the weaknesses of the cosmic design or "fine tuning" argument discussed earlier is that it relies upon a probabilistic or inductive method or reasoning.

> Perhaps the most fatal objective objection is that the cosmic design argument commits the "god of the gaps" fallacy. Because the argument is formulated as a probabilistic case for God, the natural theologian argues that God is the best explanation of the fine-tuning constants... It is not within the province of science to detect the nation of formal and final causes and is not concerned with them. Christian (and Islamic) theists might wish to see design in the deeper structures of the universe, but the scientists is methodologically constrained to seek naturalistic explanations alone.[47]

Another aspect of the modern scientific outlook is its reliance upon a mechanistic understanding of the universe and its use preventing the teleological argument for God's existence.

> The inspiration of the modern teleological argument can be traced back to the philosophy of modern thinkers such as Bacon, Galileo, Descartes, Hobbes, Boyle and Locke, who devised mechanistic conceptions of material reality. While these thinkers successfully refuted Aristotle's physics (i.e., "the earth is the center of the universe") they unfortunately equated this with a denial of his metaphysics (the act/potency distinction/ hylomorphism, etc.) Thus any refutation of Aristotelian-Thomistic metaphysics must come from within the Sphere of philosophy, not from science. [48]

Thomas Aquinas developed five proofs for the existence of God which he believed could be proven by reason and not by revelation or faith. Most of these proofs relied upon the Aristotelian understanding of the four causes – material, formal, final and efficient causality. As we have mentioned previously, modern science limits itself primarily to efficient and material causality but the Thomistic proofs rely upon the fuller understanding of the nature of causality. In the Fifth Way of Thomas Aquinas often called the argument from Intelligent Design, Thomas bases his argument not on material or efficient causality but rather on formal and final as the metaphysical foundation for the created order and avoids the "god of the gaps" rebuttal that is often used to undermine this argument. "For Aquinas, probabilistic or improbable arguments do not make sense unless it is already assumed that we live in an ordered universe.. And if we live in an ordered universe, then we need a Supreme Orderer who gives it the order that it has." [49]The ability of scientists to prove the "laws" of evolution and the unfolding universe are dependent upon the actual intelligibility of the universe given the limited range of our sense experience. The rational order or the universe can combine both lawful regularity but also Indeterminancy. Without the combination of deterministic laws and some form of freedom, we would be imprisoned in either a robotic universe or one in which chance and chaos ruled the earth and heavens. Scientists will continually seek to understand the elements of nature that can be explained using material and efficient causality but the purpose of the universe and its underlying intelligibility is the province of philosophy and religion. Both Islam and Christianity rely upon an underlying metaphysical foundation for the universe which transcends empirical observation. This foundation is the basis for sacramental understanding of nature that can be found both in the Hebrew and Christian Scriptures and the Islamic Qur'an. The modern scientific world is experiencing an ecological crisis that requires all people of good will, both secular and religious, to protect the global environment and provide a future hospitable home for all of humanity. The recent report of the Union of Concerned Scientists and the Intergovernmental Panel on Climate Change indicates that human activity is the primary cause of global climate change and global warming.[50] Science can identify many of ecological and economic challenges facing humanity but a global ethic involving representatives of the major world religions is necessary to meet this challenge within the compass of a global spiritual vision for the 21ˢᵗ century.

> We humans are inflicting deadly damage on our planet at an accelerating pace, compromising its identity as a dwelling place for life. Overconsumption, unbridled rproduction, exploitative use of resources, and efflorescing pollution are rapidly depleting life-supporting systems on land, in the sea, and in the air. The carrying capacity of the Earth is being exhausted by this human use: our species consumes resources faster than the Earth's power to replenish itself. This assault on the planet, intended or not, wreaks ecological harm of great magnitude. The unholy alliance is well known: global warming, holes in the ozone layer, clear-cut forests, drained wetlands, denuded soils, polluted air, poisoned rivers, overfished oceans, and, over all, the threat of nuclear conflagration.[51]

With the cooperation of scientists, politicians and spiritual leaders the human community can impel and propel humanity forward toward a solution of these vexing problems. Each of us bears the responsibility to join in this effort to reclaim the Earth for future generations yet unborn but that rely on us for designing polices that will reclaim and restore Mother Earth.

---

1 Armstrong, Karen. *The Case for God* (New York: Alfred Knopf, 2009), 169.

2 Brian P. Copenhagen & Charles B Schmitt *Renaissance Philosophy*. (Oxford University Press: 1992), 29. Renaissance Art also represented a turning point in the relationship of science and art. Beginning with Francis of Assisi nature began to play a more important role in western art history leading eventually to the introduction of linear perspective into western by Brunelleschi in the middle of the fifteenth century and perfected by Leonardo, Raphael and Michelangelo in the High Renaissance. See Martin Kemp's *The Science of Art* (New Have: Yale University Press, 1990). I am grateful to Rose Mewhort, a historian of western religious art for her insights into Renaissance art.

3 Armstrong, *Op.Cit.*, 169-170.

4 *Ibid.*, 171.

5 Charles Taylor. *A Secular Age* (Cambridge: Harvard University Press: 2007), 87.

6 *Ibid.*, 112.

7 *Ibid.*, 114.

8 William F. Law head. *The Voyage of Discovery: A Historical Introduction to Philosophy* (Belmont, CA: Wadsworth:

2007), 238.

9 I*bid.*, 239.

10 Daniel Kulak & Garrett Thompson. *The Longman Standard History of Philosophy* (New York: Pearson/Longman: 2006), 384.

11 Armstrong, *Op.Cit.*, 202-203.

12 *Ibid.*, 203.

13 *Ibid.*, 205.

14 Law head. *Op.Cit.*, 207.

15 *Ibid.*, 312

16 Armstrong. *Op.Cit.*, 211.

17 *Ibid.*, 213.

18 Thomas Paine. *Age of Reason. Age of Reason Introduction. http://www. ushistory.org/paine/reason/singlehtml.htm*

19 *Ibid.*, Pat First, Section 1.

20 *Ibid.*, Part First Section 1.

21 *Ibid.*, Part First Section 7.

22 Thomas Paine. "African Slavery in America," *Pennsylvania Journal and the Weekly Advertiser. April 14. 1775. http://www.constitution.org/tp/ afri.htm*

23 Thomas Paine. *Age of Reason*. Part First. Section 1.

24 Steven T. Corneliussen, Special Assistant for Science Communication, Accelerator Division. Jefferson Lab. Science Education. *http://education.jlab. org/qa/historyus_01.html*

25 US History. http://www.ushistory.org/us/26f.asp

26 Lawhead. *Op.Cit.,* 499.

27 Armstrong. *Op.Cit.,* 241.

28 Reza Aslan. *No god but God: The Origins, Evolution and Future of Islam* (Random House: New York, 2005) 226-227.

29 See my discussion of Fethullah Gulen in *Spiritual Paths to an Ethical and Ecological Global Civilization.* pages 105-110. For a discussion of "Islamic Modernism" see the treatment by John L. Esposito in *The Future of Islam* (Oxford University Press: 2010) pages 90-93.

30 Armstrong. *Op.City,* 247.

31 *Ibid.,* 246. For a contemporary discussion of Darwinism from a theological perspective, see John F. Haught's *Making Sense of Evolution: Darwin, God and the Drama of Life* (Louisville, KY: Westminster John Knox Press: 2010). See also Elizabeth Johnson's *Ask the Beast: Darwin and the God of Love* (New York: Bloomsbury, 2014).

32 Pope Pius XIX. *Divino Afflate Spiritu.* Chapter 17. *http://www.vatican.va/ holy_father/pius_xii/encyclicals/documents/hf_p-xii_enc_30091943_divino-afflante-spiritu_en.html*

33 Pierre Teilhard de Chardin. *Modern Spiritual Masters Series.* Writings Selected by Ursula King. (Orbis Books; Maryknoll, NY: 2012) 64. Fur a fuller treatment of Teilhard de Chardin's evolutionary though see also John Raymaker and Gerald Grudzen's *Spiritual Paths to an Ethical and Ecological Global Civilization* (Pacem in Terris Press: 2013). This book shows the importance of Teilhard's concepts of planetization (aka globalization), and unification for the future of a metafaith narrative. Teilhard focused more on the Christian faith in the evolutionary process but what is needed today is a narrative in which the major spiritual traditions can feel part of the story of *homo sapiens* achieving its full potential and moving together toward global unity.

34 Pierre Teilhard de Chardin., *Divine Milieu. Op.Cit.,* 72.

35 John F. Haught, *Deeper than Darwin: The Prospect for Religion in the Age of Darwin* (Boulder, CO: Westview: 2003), 6.

36 Elizabeth A. Johnson, *Quest for the Living God: Mapping Frontiers in the Theology of God,* (New York: Bloomsbury, 2007), 193-194.

37 Robert Bellah, *Religion in Human Evolution: From the Paleolithic Age to the Axial Age*, (Cambridge, Belknap: 2011), xiii.

38 Bellah, *Op.Cit.*, 9.

39 For a scholarly summary of the historical context of the life of Jesus of Nazareth, see the work of Jose Antonio Pagola, *Jesus: An Historical Approximation*, translated by Margaret Wilde, (Miami, Florida: Convivium, 2009). See particularly Appendix B, Current Methods of Research on Jesus.495-498.

40 Dennis Overbye, "Space Ripples Reveal Big Bang's Smoking Gun," *New York Times*: March 17. 2014.

41 "The Stone," *New York Times Opinion Page*, June 15, 2014.

42 *Ibid.*, Tim Maudlin

43 *Ibid.*

44 Stefano Bigliardi, "Stenmark's Multidimensional model and the Contemporary Debate on islam and Science," *Theology and Science*, (Vol 12, Number 1, February, 2014) 15-16.

45 *Ibid.*, 16.

46 *Ibid.*, 17.

47 Glenn Sinescalchi, "Fine Tuning, Atheist Criticism and the Fifty Way." *Theology and Science*, (Volume 12, Number 1, February, 2014) 69.

48 Ibid., 69-70.

49 *Ibid.*, 73

50 See the Union of Concerned Scientists web page for a summary of the latest research on global climate change and global warming: http://www.ucsusa.org/ global_warming/science_and_impacts/science/ipcc-backgrounder.html

51 Elizabeth Johnson, *Op.Cit.*, 186. For a more comprehensive discussion of the global environmental crisis from a primarily biblical perspective, see Noah Toly and Daniel Block (eds.) *Keeping God's Earth: The Global Environment in Biblical Perspective* (Downers Grove: Intervarsity Press, 2010. For an interfaith and global spiritual perspective on ecology see Mary Evelyn Tucker and John Grim's *World Views and Ecology: Religion, Philosophy and the Environment* (Marknoll: Orbis, 1994. For an Islamic perspective on the Environment see Khalid Fazul's *Islam and the Environment* (London: Ta-Ha Publishers, 1999)

Selected Bibliography

Greek and Islamic Sources of Spirituality and Science

Açkgenç, Alparslan. *Islamic Science: Towards A Definition*. Kuala Lumpur: ISTAC, 1996.

Al-Ghazali, Abu Hamid. *Mishkat al-Anwar* (The Niche for Lights). Translated by W. H. T. Gairdner. London: Royal Asiatic Society, 1924.

_____. *Al-Munqidh min al-Dalal* (Freedom and Fulfillment). Edited and annotated by R. J. McCarthy. Boston: Wayne, 1980.

_____. *The Book of Knowledge*. Translated by N. A. Faris. Lahore, Pakistan: S. M. Ashraf, 1962.

_____. *The Incoherence of the Philosophers*. Translated from Arabic by M.E. Marmura. Utah: Brigham Young University Press, 1997.

Al-Jami, Nur al-Din 'Abd al-Rahman Ibn Ahmad. *Al-Durrah al-Fakhirah* (The Precious Pearl). Translated by Nicholas Heer. Albany: State University of New York Press, 1979.

Al-Attas, Syed Muhammad Naquib. *Prolegomena to the Islamic Metaphysics of Islam: An Exposition of the Fundamental Elements of the Worldview of Islam.* Kuala Lumpur: ISTAC, 1995.

Ansari, Z. *Quranic Concepts of Human Psyche*. Islamabad, Pakistan: Islamic Research Institute Press, 1992.

Avicenna. *Kitab al-Nafs* (On the Soul). Edited by Fazlur Rahman. London: Oxford University Press, 1959.

Bakar, Osman. *Tawhid and Science: Essays on the History and Philosophy of Islamic Science*. Kuala Lumpur: Secretariat for Islamic Philosophy and Science, 1991.

Böwering, Gerhard. *The Mystical Vision of Existence in Classical Islam.* Berlin: Walter De Gruyter, 1980.

Bridges, J.H., ed. *The Opus Maius of Roger Bacon*, 2 vols. Oxford: 1897 – 1900.

Brooke, John Hedley. *Science and Religion: Some Historical Perspectives.* Cambridge: Cambridge University Press, 1991.

Bucaille, Morris. *The Bible, the Qur'an and Science.* Hinsdale, IL: North American Trust Publications, 1978.

Chittick, William C. *The Self-Disclosure of God: Principles of Ibn al-`Arabi's Cosmology.* New York: State University of New York Press, 1998.

Chittick, William C. *The Heart of Islamic Philosophy.* Oxford University Press (in production).

_____. *The Sufi Path of Knowledge: Ibn Al-Arabi's Metaphysics of Imagination.* New York: State University of New York Press, 1989.

Cohen, Morris R. and I. E. Drabkin. *A Source Book in Greek Science.* Cambridge, Mass: Harvard University Press, 1948.

Corbin. H. *Avicenna and the Visionary Recital.* New York: Pantheon, 1960.

Corey, M. A. *God and the New Cosmology: The Anthropic Design Argument.* Lanham, MD: Rowman and Littlefield Publishers, Inc., 1993.

Craig, William Lane and Quentin Smith. *Theism, Atheism, and Big Bang Cosmology.* Oxford: Clarendon Press, 1993.

Craig, William Lane. *The Kalam Cosmological Argument.* London: The Macmillan Press Ltd., 1979.

_____. *The Cosmological Argument from Plato to Leibniz.* London: The Macmillan Press Ltd, 1980.

Crombie, A. C. *Roger Grossteste and the Origins of Experimental Science: 1100-1700.* Oxford: Clarendon Press, 1953.

Crowley, T. *Roger Bacon: The Problem of the Soul in his Philosophical Commentaries.* Louvain-Dublin, 1950.

Davidson, H. A. "Alfarabi and Avicenna on the Active Intellect." *Viator 3* (1972): 109.

Dhanani, Alnoor. *The Physical Theory of Kalam: Atoms, Space, and Void in Basrian Mu'tazila's Cosmology.* Leiden: E. J. Brill, 1994.

Eaton, Charles Le Gai. *Islam and the Destiny of Man.* London: G. Allen and Unwin, 1985.

Edwards, Paul, ed. *The Encyclopaedia of Philosophy.* London: Collier and Macmillan, 1967.

Frank, Richard M. *The Metaphysics of Created Being According to Abu'l Hudhayl al- Allaf.* Istanbul: Nederlands Historisch-Archaeologisch Institute in Het Nabije Oosten, 1966.

Frank, R. *Creation and the Qu'ranic System: Al-Ghazali and Avicenna.* Heildelberg: Akademie der Wissenschaften, 1992.

Gutas, D. *Avicenna and the Aristotelian Tradition.* Leiden: E. J. Brill, 1998.

Haq, S. Nomanul. "The Indian and Persian Background." In *Routledge History of Islamic Philosophy,* edited by S. H. Nasr and O. Leaman. London: Routledge, 1996.

Hastings, James, ed. *Encyclopaedia of Religion and Ethics,* vol. II. New York: Charles Scribner's Sons, 1981.

Heinen, A. M. "Mutakallimûn and Mathematicians." *Der Islam 55* (1978): 55 – 73.

Hourani, George F., ed. *Essays on Islamic Philosophy and Science*. Albany: State University of New York Press, 1975.

Huff, Toby. *The Rise of Early Modern Science*. Cambridge: Cambridge University Press, 1993.

Ibn Arabi. *Fusus al-Hikam* (The Wisdom of the Prophets). Translated by Titus Burckhardt and Angela Culme-Seymour. London: Concord Grove Press, 1983.

Iraqi, Fakhruddin. *Divine Flashes*. Translation and introduction by William Chittick. New York: Paulist Press, 1982.

Izutsu, Toshihiko. *God and Man in the Koran: Semantics of the Koranic Weltanschauung*. Tokyo: The Keio Institute of Cultural and Linguistic Studies, 1964.

Jevons, W. Stanley. *Elementary Lessons in Logic*. London: Macmillan, 1882.

Kraemer, Joel L. *Humanism in the Renaissance of Islam*. Leiden, New York and Köln: E. J. Brill, 1992.

Lane, Edward William. *An Arabic-English Lexicon*. Beirut: Librairie Du Liban, 1968.

Lerner, Ralph and Mushin Mahdi, eds. *Medieval Political Thought: A Sourcebook*. Canada: The Free Press of Clencoe Colliermacmillan Limited, 1963.

Lewis, T. Charlton et al, ed. *A Latin Dictionary* (based on Andrew's edition of Fround's *Latin Dictionary*). Oxford, New York: 1879.

Lings, Martin. *The Book of Certainty*. Lahore, Pakistan: Suhail Academy, 1999.

Little, A. G, ed. *Roger Bacon: Essays Contributed by Various Authors on the Occasion of the Commemoration of the Seventh Centenary of His Birth*. Oxford, 1914.

Massignon, Louis. *The Passion of al-Hallaj*, 4 vols. Translated by Herbert Mason. Princeton: Princeton University Press, 1982.

Morewedge, P. *Neo-Platonism and Islamic Thought*. Albany: SUNY Press, 1992.

Morse, Joseph Laffan, ed. *Funk and Wagnalls Standard Reference Encyclopaedia*, vol. 3. New York: Standard Reference Works, 1959.

Morris, James, W. *The Wisdom of the Throne: An Introduction to the Philosophy of Mulla Sadra*. Princeton: Princeton University Press, 1981.

Murata, Sachicko. *Tao of Islam*. New York: State University of New York Press, 1992.

Murata, Sachiko and William Chittick. *The Vision of Islam*. St. Paul, MN: Paragon House, 1995.

Muttahari, Mortaza. *Tawheed Qum: Intesharat-e Sadra*, 1373.

Nasr, Seyyed Hossein. *Science and Civilization in Islam*. Chicago: ABC International Group, 2001.

_____. *Islamic Life and Thought* (reprint). Lahore: Suhail Academy, 1999.

_____. *An Introduction to Islamic Cosmological Doctrines*. Cambridge: The Belknap Press of Harvard University Press, 1964.

Nasr, Seyyed Hossein and Oliver Leaman, eds. *History of Islamic Philosophy* (Routledge History of World Philosophies). New York: State University of New York Press, 1987.

Northbourne, Lord. *Looking Back on Progress* (reprint). Lahore: Suhail Academy, 1999.

North, D. John. "Roger Bacon and the Saracens" in *Filosofia e scienza classica, arabo-latina medievale e l'età moderna. Ciclo di seminari internazionali (26-27 gennaio 1996)*, ed. G. Federici Vescovini, Textes et Études du Moyen Âge 11 (Louvain-la-Neuve, 1999), 129 – 160.

Nusseibeh, S. "Al-Aql al-Qudsz: Avicenna's Subjective Theory of Knowledge." *Studia Islamica*, 49 (1989): 39 – 54.

Ormsby, Eric L. *Theodicy in Islamic Thought*. Princeton: Princeton University Press, 1984.

Oxford English Dictionary, vol. IX. Oxford: Oxford University Press, 1961.

Pervez, Hoodbhoy. *Islam and Science*. London: Zed, 1991.

Piamenta, M. *The Muslim Conception of God and Human Welfare*. Leiden: E.J. Brill, 1983.

Plessner, M. *The Natural Sciences and Medicine in the Legacy of Islam*, second edition. Edited by J. Schacht and E. Bosworth. Oxford: The Clarendon Press, 1974.

Presidency of Islamic Researches, revisers and editors. *Holy Qu'ran: English Translation of Meaning and Commentary*. Medina: King Fahad Holy Qu'ran Printing Complex, 1992.

Qashairi, Abu'l Qasim, and Abdul Karim bin Hawazan. *Rasala Qashairiah*, second edition. Translated from Urdu by Dr. Pir Muhammad Hasan. Islamabad: Islamic Research Institute, 1988.

Rahbar, Daud. *God of Justice: A Study in the Ethical Doctrine of the Qur'an*. Leiden: E.J. Brill, 1960.

Rahman, Fazlur. *Islam*. London: Weidenfeld and Nicolson, 1966.

Raschid, M. S. *Iqbal's Concept of God*. London: Kegan Paul International, 1981.

Rashed, R. "Problems of the Transmission of Greek Scientific Thought into Arabic: Examples from Mathematics and Optics." *History of Science 27* (1989).

Razi, Fakh al-Din. *al-Matalib al-Aliyah min al-Ilm al-Ilahi*, vol. 4. Beirut: Dar al- Kitab al-Arabi, 1987.

Rescher, Nicholas. *Studies in Arabic Philosophy*. Pittsburgh: University of Pittsburgh Press, 1966

Richardson, J. *Dictionary: Persian, Arabic and English*. London: 1806.

Rizwi, Azhar Ali. *Muslim Contributions to Psychotherapy*. Lahore: University of Punjab Press, 1987.

Sabra, A. I. "The Appropriation and Subsequent Naturalization of Greek Science in Medieval Islam." *History of Science 25* (1987): 223 – 243.

Saliba, Saliba. *A History of Arabic Astronomy: Planetary Theories During the Golden Age of Islam*. New York: New York University Press, 1994.

Sarton, George. *Introduction to the History of Science*. Baltimore, MD: Williams and Wilkins, 1962.

Schuon, Frithjof. *Understanding Islam*. London: Allen and Unwin, 1963.

Sharif, M. M., ed. *A History of Muslim Philosophy*. Wiesbaden: Otto Harrassowitz, 1963.

Shehadi, Fadlou. *Metaphysics in Islamic Philosophy*. New York: Caravan Books, 1982.

Smith, Huston. *Forgotten Truth*. Lahore: Suhail Academy, 1981.

_____. *Beyond the Postmodern Mind*. New York: Crossroads, 1989.

Smith, Jane Idleman, trans. *Al-Durra al-Fakhira* (The Precious Pearl). Missoula, MT: Scholars Press, 1979.

Southern. R.W. *Western Views of Islam in the Middle Ages.* Cambridge, MA: Harvard University Press, 1962.

Stenberg, Leif. *The Islamization of Science: Four Muslim Positions Developing an Islamic Modernity* (Lund Studies in History of Religions). New York: Coronet Books, 1996.

Thorndike, L. *A History of Magic and Experimental Science,* vol.1. New York: Columbia University Press, 1923 – 1958.

Townsend, P.N., trans. *Dimensions of Islam.* London: Allen and Unwin, 1966.

Ullah, Mohammad Zia. *The Islamic Concept of God.* London: Kegan Paul International, 1984.

Ullmann, M. *Islamic Medicine,* Islamic Surveys II (14). Edinburgh: Edinburgh University Press, 1978.

Waheed, Khwaja Abdul. *Islam and the Origins of Modern Science.* Lahore: Islamic Publications Ltd., 1978.

Watt, Montgomery. *The Formative Period of Islamic Thought.* Edinburgh: The University Press, 1973.

Woodburn, John. "Science Defined Versus Indefinable, A Personal Attempt to Define Science." *The Science Teacher 34, no. 8* (Nov. 1967): 23 – 30.

Christian Sources of Spirituality and Science

Alfano, Archbishop of Salerno. *De Quattuor Humoribus Corporis Humani.* Edited by F. Caparoni. Rome, 1928. Located at the New York Academy of Medicine (NYAM).

Amundsen, Darrel and Ronald Numbers, eds. *Caring and Curing: Health and Medicine in the Western Religious Traditions.* New York: Macmillan, 1986.

Beccaria, Augustino. *I codici di medicina del periodo presalernitana* (secoli IX, X, e XI). Rome: Edizioni di Storia e Letteratura, 1956.

Benson, Robert L. and Giles Constable with Carl D. Lanham, eds. *Renaissance and Renewal in the Twelfth Century.* Cambridge: Harvard University Press, 1982.

Bloch, Herbert. *Monte Cassino in the Middle Ages,* 3 vols. Cambridge: Harvard University Press, 1986.

Bullough, Vern. *The Development of Medicine as a Profession: The Contribution of the Medieval University to Modern Medicine.* New York: Harpers, 1966.

Burnett, Charles. "Encounters with Razi the Philosopher: Constantine the African, Petrus Alfonsi and Ramon Marti." *Pensamiento Medieval Hispano: Homenaje a Horacio Santiago-Otero* (1998). J.M.Soto Rabanos, ed.

Burnett, Charles and Danielle Jacquart, eds. *Constantine the African and Ali al Abbas al- Magusi: The Pantegni and Related Texts.* London: Brill, 1994.

Burnett, Charles. "The Contents and Affiliations of the Scientific Manuscripts Written At, or Brought to, Chartres in the Time of John of Salisbury." In *The World of John of Salisbury,* edited by Michale Wilks. Oxford: Blackwell, 1984).

_____. "Physics Before the Physics: Early Translations from Arabic of Texts Concerning Nature in MSS British Library Additional 22719 and Cotton Galba E IV." *Medioevo: Revista Di Storis Della Filosofia Medievale. XXVII* (2002).

Corner, George Washington. *Anatomical Texts of the Earlier Middle Ages: A Study in the Transmission of Culture.* Washington, D.C.: Carnegie Institute of Washington, 1929.

Cowdrey, H.E.J. *The Age of Abbot Desiderius, Montecassino, the Papacy and theNormans in the Eleventh and Early Twelfth Centuries.* Oxford: Clarendon Press,1983.

Creutz, R. "Der Arzt Constantino Africanus von Montecassino: Sein leber, sein Werk und Sein Bedeutung, fur die mittelalterliche medizinische Wissenschaft." *StudienUnd Mitteilvagen der Benedictaner Oriens XLVII* (1931): 25 – 44.

_____. "Erzbishof Alfano I, ein frusalerntanischer Arzt." *Studien und Mitteilvagen Der Benediktaner Ordens. XLVII* (1929): 413 – 432.

DeRenzi, Salvatore. *Collectio Salerntana ossia documenta inedita e trattati di medicina appartenti alla scuola medica salernitana* 5 vols. Naples: Filatre-Sabezio, 1852 – 59: reprint: Bologna: Forni, 1967.

Getz, Faye. "The Faculty of Medicine before 1500." In *The History of the University of Oxford*, T.H. Ashton, General Editor. Vol 2: *Late Medieval Oxford*, edited by J.L.Cato and Ralph Evans. Oxford: Clarendon Press, 1922.

Grant, Edward, ed. *A Source Book in Medieval Science.* Cambridge, MA: Harvard University Press, 1974.

Green, Monica H., ed. and trans. *The Trotula: An English Translation of the Medieval Compendium of Women's Medicine.* Philadelphia: University of Pennsylvania Press, 2001.

Haskins, Charles Homer. *The Rise of the Universities.* New York: H. Holt, 1923.

_____. *Studies in the History of Medieval Science.* Cambridge:Harvard University Press, 1923.

Jacquart, Danielle. "Le sens donne par Constantin l'Africain a son oeuvre: les chapitres introductifs en arabe et en latin." In *Constantine the African and Ali Ibn Al-Abbas Al-Magusi: The Pantegni and Related Texts*, edited by Charles Burnett and Danielle Jacquart. Leiden: Brill, 1994, 71 – 89.

_____. "Aristotelian Thought in Salerno." In *A History of Twelfth Century Western Philosophy*, edited by Peter Dronke. Cambridge: Cambridge University Press, 1988.

_____. "The Introduction of Arabic Medicine into the West: The Question of Etiology." In *Health, Disease and Healing in Medieval Culture*, edited by Sheila Campbell, Brent Hall and David Klausner. Basingstoke, UK: Macmillan, 1991,, 186 – 195

Jacaquart, Danielle and Francoise Micheau. *La Médicine Arabe et L'Occident Médiéval.* Paris: Editions Maissonneuve and Larose, 1990.

Jordan, Mark D. "The Fortune of Constantine's Pantegni." In *Constantine the African and Ali Ibn Al-Abbas Al-Magusi: The Pantegni and Related Texts*, edited by Charles Burnett and Danielle Jacquart. Leiden: Brill, 1994.

_____. "Medicine as Science in the Early Commentaries of Johannitius," *Traditio XLIII* (1987): 121 – 145.

_____. "The Construction of a Philosophical Medicine: Exegesis and Argument in Salnernitan Teaching on the Soul." *Osiris 6*, 2nd Series (1990): 42 – 61.

Kibre, Pearl. *Hippocrates Latinus: Repertorium of Hippocratic Writings in the Latin Middle Ages*, revised edition. New York: Fordham University Press, 1985.

Kristeller, Paul Oscar. "The School of Salerno: Its Development and its Contribution to The History of Learning." In *Studies in Renaissance Thought and Letters*, 494 – 551. Rome: Edizioni di Storia e Letteratura, 1956.

_____. "Bartholomaeus, Musandino and Maurus of Salerno and Other Early Commentators on the _Articella_ with a Tentative List of Texts and Manuscripts." _Italia Medioevale e Umanistica_ 19 (1967): 57 – 87. Revised Italian edition in _Studi Scuola Medica Salernitana_. Napoli: Instituto Italiano per gli studi filosofici, 1986.

Lawn, Brian. _The Salnernitan Questions: An Introduction to the History of Medieval and Renaissance Problem Literature_. Oxford: Clarendon Press, 1963.

_____. _The Prose Salernitan Questions_. London: British Academy/Oxford University Press, 1979.

Lindberg, David. _The Beginnings of Western Science: The European Tradition in Philosophical, Religious and Institutional Context: 600 B.C. to AD 1450_. Chicago: University of Chicago Press, 1992.

Mackinney, Loren. _Medical Illustrations in Medieval Manuscripts_. Berkeley: University of California Press, 1965.

McVaugh, Michael. "Constantine the African." In _Dictionary of Scientific Biography, vol 3_, edited by Charles Gillispie. New York: Scribners, 1970, 393 – 395.

_____. "History of Medicine." In _Dictionary of the Middle Ages, vol. 8_, edited by Joseph Stranger. New York: Scribners, 1987.
Newton, Francis. "The Scriptorium and Library at Montecassino: 1058-1109." _Cambridge Studies in Paleography and Codicology 7_: 1999.

Nutton, Vivian. _From Democedes to Harvey_. London: Variorum Reprints, 1968.

_____. _Ancient Medicine_. London: Routledge, 2004.

O'Boyle, Cornelius. _The Art of Medicine: Medical Teaching at the University of Paris_. London: Brill, 1998.

Siclari, Alberto. *L'Antropologia di Nemesio di Emesa*. Parma: Editrice "La Garangola," 1974.

Singer, Charles and Dorothea Singer. "The Origins of the Medical School of Salerno, the First University: An Attempted Reconstruction". In *Essays on the History of Medicine Presented to Karl Sudhoff*, edited by Charles Singer and Henry Sigerist. Zurich: Seldwyn, 1924.

Siraisi, Nancy G. "The Faculty of Medicine." In *History of the Universities in the Middle Ages*, edited by Hilde de Ridder-Symoens. Cambridge: Cambridge University Press, 1992, 360 – 387.

_____. *Medieval and Early Renaissance Medicine: An Introduction to Knowledge and Practice*. Chicago: University of Chicago Press, 1990.

Telfer, William, ed. *The Library of Christian Classics*. XIII vols. vol. IV, *Cyril of Jerusalem and Nemesius of Emesa*. Philadelphia: The Westminster Press, 1955.

Thorndyke, Lynn. *A History of Magic and Experimental Science*, 8 volumes. London:Macmillan, 1923.

Thorndyke, Lynn and Pearl Kibre. *A Catalogue of Incipits of Medieval Scientific Manuscripts in Latin*, revised and augmented edition. Cambridge, MA: Medieval Academy of America, 1963.

Ullman, Manfred. *Islamic Medicine*. Edinburgh: Edinburgh University Press, 1978.

Wack, Mary F. *Lovesickness in the Middle Ages: The "Viaticum" and Its Commentaries*. Philadelphia: University of Pennsylvania, 1990.

Wilks, Michael, editor. "The Contents and Affiliation of the Scientific Manuscripts Written at, or Brought to Chartres, in the Time of John of Salisbury." In *Studies in Church History*, 127 – 160. Oxford: Blackwell, 1984.

Gerald J. Grudzen, PhD

Doctor Grudzen earned his PhD in intellectual history from Columbia University in New York with a specialization in Christian and Islamic philosophy and medical science. Edwin Mellen Press published Grudzen's *Medical Theory About the Body and Soul in the Middle Ages in 2007*. This book examines the history of medical philosophy from the time of Galen around 200 CE to the emergence of the first western medical curriculum in 1100 CE. His study shows the intedependence of Jewish, Christian and Islamic medical and philosophical scholarship during the early medieval era from 750 CE to 1100 CE. Grudzen teaches Philosophy and Comparative Religion for San Jose City College and the University of Phoenix at its Bay Area campuses and its national Online program. Grudzen received a Templeton Foundation award through the Graduate Thelogical Union's Center for Theology and the Natural Sciences (CTNS) to develop a religion and science curriculum with both Christian and Islamic Perspectives. Grudzen also has participated in programs on religion and science offered at the Ian Ramsey Centre of Oxford University and CTNS of Berkeley, California.

AKA Shamsur Rahman, PhD

Doctor Rahman has been a Commonwealth Fellow doing post-doctoral research at Harris Manchester College, Oxford University, from 2002 to 2006 under the direction of John Hedley Brooke, Director of the Ian Ramsey Centre for Science and Religion. He earned his PhD in Philosophy from the University of Reading, United Kingdom. He worked as Chairperson of the Department of Philosophy at the University of Chittagong prior to his appointment as a Commonwealth Fellow in the UK. Doctor Rahman collaborated with Doctor Grudzen in the development of a curriculum in the history of medieval and early modern philosophy and science from the perspective of Islamic and Christian faith traditions funded by the John Templeton Foundation. Their joint text, *Spirituality and Science,* has been developed over several years of collaboration. Doctor Rahman chaired an international religion and science conference in January of 2008 in Dhaka, Bangladesh sponsored by several international religious and academic organizations, which he and Doctor Grudzen organized.

CPSIA information can be obtained
at www.ICGtesting.com
Printed in the USA
FSOW01n1833020917
38282FS